FREE YOUR PEN

Mind Training for Writers

54 Slogans to
Cure Writer's Block
& Free Your Voice

Jessica Davidson

JesDharma Books

Cover © 2017 Jessica Davidson
Photo by Yosep Sugiarto

Published by JesDharma Books
Printed by CreateSpace
www.jessicadavidson.co.uk

Contents

Appendix

Introduction

Congratulations! You have taken the first step on the path to master your thoughts and get your mind to behave itself.

Free Your Pen is for writers who struggle to write, as well as those who don't. Whether you're happy with your writing but would like to go deeper, or feel blocked creatively, this book will help.

Free Your Pen gives you a practical system of meditation designed to free your mind from distractions and emotional blocks, based on the Buddhist practice of lojong. Working with the 59 slogans in this book will help to shut down your inner critic and dissolve the fears and limitations that can block your writing.

This book will help you:

- To find your voice and free your mind
- To write courageously with self-knowledge
- To be authentic
- To become the writer you were born to be

How to Use This Book

The 59 slogans in this book come from the lojong tradition of Tibetan Buddhism. Lojong simply means 'mind training' and the slogans are easy to remember phrases that encourage and challenge you to turn towards your problems rather than avoiding them. It's a simple, down-to-earth technique for making friends with yourself.

You can use the techniques in this book to dissolve your fears and root out the emotional problems that interrupt the flow and get yourself writing again. You can also use it to transform your creative work into a spiritual practice, and your writing into a vehicle to explore your mind and deepen your engagement with life.

The book is divided into two sections. In Part One we look at some of the ideas behind mind training and why it is so important. Chapter One explores the reasons we become blocked and identifies the root cause in the structures of the ego and shadow. Chapter Two has a closer look at the tradition of lojong and some of the essential ideas that underpin the practice. Chapter Three goes into detail about how to work with the slogans and offers some practical suggestions.

Part Two introduces each of the slogans and looks at how you can apply them to your life and writing practice. Every slogan includes practical exercises so you can explore them for yourself and put the ideas into practice. Finally, the Appendix includes a handy glossary of terms, details on the original slogans, plus references and resources for you to explore the practice further.

You don't have to be a Buddhist to benefit from this book. You don't even have to meditate on the slogans, if you don't want to. It's simply a way to become more present in your life, to pay attention to what you're feeling and thinking, and to come alive.

May your pen and your mind be free!

Part One

Understanding
Mind Training

~

4   FREE YOUR PEN

Chapter 1: Why Train the Mind?

Have you ever sat down to write and found that your mind has gone totally blank? Or you know what you want to say, but there are so many words bouncing around inside your head that you don't know where to start?

When you try to write without focusing your mind it's like stepping into an echo chamber with all the usual suspects shouting at once. You might manage to write through the hubbub and eventually it will settle down, but there are times when the noise takes over. When that happens, the writing stops.

Trying to write through blockages and distractions is no fun. But there is a way to take back control and create some space in your mind so you can focus: mind training!

It sounds boring – and hard work – but mind training could be the key to tapping into the power of your mind.

As a writer, your mind is your most valuable resource. But if your mind is full of doubts and distractions, you won't be able to express yourself clearly. That's where mind training comes in. It can help you to shut down the annoying inner critic, dissolve your fears, transcend your limitations, and reconnect with the parts of yourself that get lost in the hustle and jumble of daily life.

The trouble is, you probably take your mind for granted. Most of the time you don't even notice it's there. You just think and worry and dream and think some more. Sometimes it all gets too much and you don't know what to think.

When your mind gets overwhelmed like this, it starts to tell lies. If you believe those lies, you might stop writing altogether. This is because of one simple truth:

It's easier not to write than it is to write.

If your stressed out mind can convince you to give up, you probably will because it's easier than fighting the problem. So you need to be proactive. You must protect your most valuable resource and take care of it. You can't write without your mind. Unfortunately, your mind is also the source of most of your problems.

Many things can block your writing or slow you down. Some come from outside: distractions, time constraints, and other practical concerns, such as family and work responsibilities. While others come from within: self-doubt, fears, negative thinking, and emotional blind spots, or physical challenges such as insomnia and illness.

Whatever you think is causing the problem, the real obstacle to taking control of your writing comes from within. Even when you believe the difficulty lies outside, it's your attitude towards it that is really causing the problem. Approached the right way, external obstacles can make you more creative because you have to think of ways to overcome the problem in order to write. So external blocks can usually be managed with a little willpower, organisation, and time management.

Internal blocks are harder to manage, partly because they're invisible. You may not even realise you have a problem until you sit down to write and nothing happens. Fears and anxieties can hide behind other problems, making it hard to see where the real difficulty lies. For example, you may think you don't have time to write, but in reality that's an excuse to avoid confronting your self-doubt.

Even when you do manage to write, the process of creating a piece of writing is fraught with anxiety. To create you must step into the unknown. You have to question the work and doubt your choices, even when the writing is going well. Is your story any good? Are you working on the right ideas? Will anybody want to read what you have written? Can you even write?

You won't be able to write anything unless you're willing to deal with the fears that arise when you create. With this in mind, it's a good idea to understand where these myriad anxieties come from. Perhaps then you can find a solution.

Meet Your Mind

Although everybody writes for different reasons, the fears that can stop you writing all spring from the same source: ego.

First, some definitions. The words ego and self tend to be used interchangeably, but they actually refer to different ideas. In psychology the ego and the self are seen as having different functions within the psyche. The self is the first to develop and gives you the sense of being located in a body with sensations and feelings. The self is an embodied experience, rooted in the awareness of your physical being.

The ego develops later, starting around age seven, and is fully formed by the time you're a young adult. The ego is a mental structure, created in relation to your physical sense of self. So the ego is what you think about your self.

It's the ego that comes up with the stories you tell yourself about who you think you are, or think you should be. Ego statements always begin with "I am," so are often called I-statements: I am a woman, I am a writer, I am your friend, I am happy, and so on.

A healthy ego is grounded through being connected to a strong sense of self. Who you think you are (ego) matches who you feel yourself to be (self) and others will perceive you this way too. This is the ideal. However, if you become too identified with your ego at the expense of your self, problems can arise.

Sometimes the ego denies too much of the reality of the body and its feelings and you lose touch with your deeper self. In extreme cases, this causes a condition called narcissism where there is a strong ego but a weak sense of self. Who you think you are doesn't match how you really feel, so much so that you may avoid feeling anything too deeply at all.

But even a healthy ego isn't perfect because as the ego is formed it creates a shadow. You can't have an ego without a shadow; they arrive together, like conjoined twins. The ego polices the conscious mind and banishes anything that it decides is unacceptable into the subconscious. This can include positive traits and potentials, as well as the more obvious negative ones that give rise to phobias, compulsions, and obsessions.

As C.G. Jung describes it, "*The shadow personifies everything that the subject refuses to acknowledge about himself and yet is always thrusting itself upon him directly or indirectly – for instance, inferior traits of character and other incompatible tendencies.*"

You push things you don't like about yourself into the basement where they become part of the shadow. But these characteristics or qualities don't disappear once they have been banished. The psyche is a dynamic system in a state of constant change and the shadow will always compensate for imbalances in the conscious mind by trying to redress the balance. So if you go too far to one extreme, the shadow will try to bring the psyche back into balance by forcing you to face what you have denied. These shadow eruptions can either occur within your own mind and body in the form of physical illness or emotional and mental distress, or they will appear in the outside world in the form of projections.

Whatever happens, your ego finds this whole process to be incredibly challenging. It has already decided that these things are unacceptable, so when they start to resurface, the ego thinks it's under attack and resists. It might even push back and fight to protect itself. This is because the ego doesn't care about wholeness or balance, it wants to be safe and in control. But the psyche doesn't care about safety or control; it seeks wholeness.

You experience this tug of war within your mind as doubts, fears, and emotional blockages. As long as you continue to resist the process of returning your psyche to balance and wholeness, you will encounter difficulties in your life. Your ego will continue to tell distorted stories about who you think you are, and it's these stories that get in the way when you're trying to write and express your true voice.

Perhaps the solution is to tell better stories. Maybe if you change the way you think about yourself, the doubt and fear will vanish. For example, replace the belief, "*I have nothing interesting to say,*" with, "*I am fascinating and erudite!*" And the problem will be solved.

Unfortunately, transforming your fears isn't that easy. To change the way you think about yourself you need to confront the underlying cause, and this can be found in the nature of the ego itself.

Because the ego has no real substance – it's just a thought, after all – it tries to make itself more solid by identifying with other things. The trouble is, everything the ego attaches itself to is prone to change. Thoughts and emotions come and go. The body ages, suffers illness and eventually dies. The roles you play in life change over time, the people you love can leave or die. Everything you rely on to make you feel safe will come to an end.

Where there is ego there is fear. To compensate for this insecurity you try to control things as much as you can, but this desire for security is doomed to fail. You cannot make permanent what is always changing.

Buddhism describes the root of all suffering as ego-grasping, a constant craving for security. The ego keeps a tight hold on itself and this has the effect of separating you from the flow of life. It's a contraction against reality that feels like a kind of mental cramp, as if your mind is a closed fist – always tense, always turning away, always saying no.

When you believe you are separate from life, you feel scared of life, and a lot of your energy and thought will go into building defences against what you fear. This is what I call the **Ego Fort**, behind whose walls you tremble in fear. And it's this fear that fuels the stories you tell yourself.

In light of all this, it's no surprise that you occasionally find it hard to write.

The Courage to Write

Writing is a leap of faith. You never really know what you're doing but it can give a great sense of purpose, structure and meaning to your life. It's a way to express joy, curiosity, amazement, and awe of this mysterious process we call life. Writing creates order out of chaos and helps to make sense of your experience. But it also involves confronting yourself and telling the truth about what you see.

Because of this, writing takes real courage. It's a risky business, not just in terms of how you might make a living, but on a personal level. You're exposing yourself, revealing your soul on the page, and that is something guaranteed to give your ego chills.

To write well you must think well. But you must also know when to stop thinking. To find your voice as a writer you need to cultivate inner silence. You need to be quiet enough inside so you can listen, not just to the still small voice of your intuition, but to your shadow voices too. The shadow provides the raw material that you transform into new ideas and creative breakthroughs. It's often seen as a dark and murky place, but it also contains hidden gems. These gems are your inner gold, your hidden talents and gifts.

Both the gold and the darkness contribute to your voice as a writer. But to access both, you need to know yourself. You need to hear your own voice through the noise and chatter of other people's voices, expectations and assumptions, and your own fears, doubts, expectations, hopes and dreams.

You need to discern the difference between the fearful voice of your ego and the voice of your true Self. You will have to let go of the writer you think you want to be in order to become the writer that you are.

To find the courage to write and clear the blocks that get in your way, you will need to practice some kind of regular mental house cleaning. Your mind should become a sanctuary; an open, spacious place that you don't fear to enter because you have made friends with it and the voices that live there. When you make friends with yourself, nothing that lurks in your subconscious can erupt and sidetrack you from writing.

As a writer, you may be able to control reality on the page, but you can't control real life quite so easily. However, you can control your response to what happens. You don't have to be stuck with dysfunctional patterns of thought or behaviour that block the expression of your deeper Self. The mind is very adaptable and it can be trained. You can free yourself from negativity and self-doubt and dissolve your fears – not by forcing them into silence, but by listening and opening to the darker side of yourself with compassion and understanding.

You may find yourself resisting the very idea of training your mind because it sounds serious. The word 'training' conjures ideas of strict discipline and boring hard work. But this resistance is just your ego talking. You will need to challenge some deeply ingrained habits, and it will take discipline, but it doesn't have to be hard work. It might even be fun!

Mind training isn't about being perfect or always knowing what to do and being in control all the time. That's the way of the ego.

Mind training is about meeting life on its own terms rather than imposing your beliefs on reality and trying to make life conform to your wishes. It's about being awake and alive and fully present to your experience, whatever it may bring. You can't know everything. Life is unpredictable and messy and you'll never get it right all the time. Training your mind is a way to make peace with yourself and life as it actually is, rather than struggling against it.

When you free your mind, your pen will follow.

Chapter 2: What is Lojong?

Lojong is a meditation practice from the Tibetan Buddhist tradition that uses 59 slogans or aphorisms to train the mind in compassion and resilience. It is rooted in the Buddha's teachings and includes practices that work as antidotes to the negative thought patterns that cause suffering.

The word *lojong* is usually translated as 'mind training', but the meaning of the Tibetan word is closer to 'refining' than to 'training' the mind. The idea is to use meditation to tame and quieten your mind, and then you can train it and refine how you think and act.

The original slogans were passed down as part of an oral tradition of teachings that began in India with the Buddha. Bengali spiritual master Atisha Dipankara brought the slogans to Tibet in 1044. The Tibetan King, Yeshe-Ö, was keen to learn more about Buddhism and invited Atisha to come and spread the Dharma.

Unsure whether he should go, Atisha prayed to the female Bodhisattva Green Tara for guidance. She appeared in a dream and told Atisha that if he went to Tibet it would extend the life of the Dharma, but his own life would be cut short. He was already in his 60s but decided the teachings were more important than his own life, so he undertook the arduous trek across the Himalayas on foot.

Atisha spent the rest of his life in Tibet spreading the teachings, but they weren't written down until a century later when Chekawa Yeshe Dorje rediscovered them. He gathered the 59 slogans into their current form in his commentary *The Root Text of the Seven Points of Training the Mind.* Many more translations and commentaries have been written since, from around the world. If you would like to explore some of them, you will find references and resources in the appendix.

For this book, I've used my own versions of some of the slogans to make them more accessible to writers and easier to remember. You can see the original slogans listed in the appendix. As we explore the teachings, you'll notice there are a few Buddhist terms to get to grips with, but don't worry, I'll explain the important ones as we go. If you forget what they mean, you can check the glossary (also in the appendix) for the definitions.

Before looking at the slogans in detail, it's worth putting them into context and exploring some of the central teachings that underpin the practice of lojong.

Mind training sounds like a very cerebral activity, but it's not just about getting your wayward mind under control. It's also about what you do with your heart. Mind training dissolves your attachment to your ego and that has the effect of opening up your heart. It stops you getting caught in your ego's stories and helps you to shift your perspective and reframe your experience. As your heart softens, you become more open and friendly, not just towards yourself, but to others too.

At the centre of lojong practice is the idea of using your problems to develop compassion, or bodhicitta, and this is achieved through the meditation practice of tonglen. Let's explore what these terms mean.

Bodhicitta

In the traditional system of teachings, the slogans are divided into seven sections or points, each one building on the last. The first two points introduce the foundational teachings, while the remaining points take you through how to apply the teachings in your daily life.

The foundation of the practice is cultivating bodhicitta, which is divided into two types: absolute (or ultimate) bodhicitta, and relative bodhicitta.

Bodhicitta is the desire to awaken to your Buddha nature in order to help others to do the same. The Pali word *bodhi* means enlightenment, while *citta* means mind, so bodhicitta is usually translated as 'enlightened or awakened mind and heart.' You might also see it spelt 'bodhichitta' because this is how it is pronounced.

Absolute bodhicitta is your true nature or Buddha mind. This is the ground of your being, the fundamental consciousness beyond all concepts before it becomes split into 'I' and 'other,' or subject and object. Absolute bodhicitta can also be called emptiness or *shunyata*,

Buddha nature, and ultimate reality. At the level of absolute bodhicitta, all is one and perceived as interconnected and interdependent. This is the goalless goal on the path to enlightenment. It is clear, open and spacious, a state of innate wakefulness or pure awareness.

While absolute bodhicitta is the foundation of wisdom and basic goodness, **relative bodhicitta** is compassion and love in action. It brings the teachings down to earth and puts them into practice in your daily life. Relative bodhicitta is about being kind to yourself and others based on the knowledge that there is no real separation between you. The realisation of bodhicitta dissolves the defences of your ego and opens your heart.

In lojong, relative bodhicitta is practised using a meditation called tonglen, which is also known as 'sending and receiving.'

Tonglen

Tonglen is a Tibetan Buddhist meditation where you breathe in suffering and breathe out compassion. At first glance, this seems counterintuitive because it's the opposite of what you would normally do when you're in pain or unhappy. But the practice is about developing compassion so the idea is to move towards your pain rather than avoiding it. This helps to keep your heart open and transforms your suffering into happiness.

Tonglen is practised for yourself and for others, and involves recognising that everybody suffers in the same way. It dissolves the boundaries that the ego places between the self and others, and this gives rise to compassion.

Tonglen uses your problems as the raw material to awaken compassion for others and heal your own wounds at the same time. Compassion isn't about feeling sorry for people, or wallowing in self-pity. It isn't even about doing good works and helping those who are less fortunate. As Norman Fischer explains in *Training in Compassion*:

> *"Compassion, for instance, sounds like such a good idea, but the problem with it is that it will probably make us sentimental, softheaded, and overly enthusiastic, and this will tend to make us troublesome to exactly the people we want*

to have compassion for, because our excessive sentimentality and insistence on being helpful will probably be annoying and counterproductive. ... Also, quite possibly, our compassion will cause us to be disapproving or even hostile to others who we are certain are not as compassionate as we are. This, of course, is the opposite of compassion. Asked about what compassion really is, an old Zen master said, 'It's like reaching back for your pillow in the dark.' In other words, it's a simple and natural human act, no big deal."

This is why lojong encourages you to develop awareness of absolute bodhicitta before you start spreading your love around. You may want to help others in a practical way as a result of doing this practice, but it's important not to fool yourself about your motives. That doesn't mean you shouldn't help others, it's just a reminder to check your true intentions.

The practice of tonglen is explored in depth in Slogan 7 and Slogan 10.

Buddha Mind

As we've seen, absolute bodhicitta is your true nature or Buddha mind, waiting patiently for you to remember who you are and come home to yourself. But what does that actually mean?

We have a confusion of selves. There is the self and the ego, and now we need to introduce another, the Self.

As we saw in Chapter One, the self (small s) tends to be confused with the ego, but they refer to different levels of experience. The ego is what you think about yourself, while the self is how it feels to be you. The Self (capital S) refers to the idea of the Higher Self, but just to confuse matters even more, it isn't really a self at all.

The Self is your Buddha mind, and has a multitude of other names: Higher Self, True Self, Pure Self, Transpersonal Self, Transcendental Self, Atman, Christ Consciousness, True Nature, Big Mind, Buddha nature, and just to make sure you get the point, the Non-Self.

The Self is seen as an archetype of wholeness in Jungian psychology. It's the root of your awareness, and has no content and no form, just like all archetypes. In psychological terms, the Higher Self tends to be in the shadow, hidden behind the thick walls of your Ego Fort. Meditation and lojong practice help to dissolve those walls and make your Self more accessible.

But in truth, the Self is always there. It is pure consciousness or awareness, and is what enables you to be aware of yourself and everything you experience. It's totally impersonal and beyond concepts, which is why it isn't strictly accurate to call it a Self – hence, the non-self of Buddhist philosophy.

Whether you call it the Self, non-self, Buddha mind, absolute bodhicitta, or emptiness, it's the same as the true nature of reality. This means that your Higher Self is the same as everybody else's Higher Self because there's no separation.

No matter what your current state of mind, you are already pure awareness in your deepest Self. The teachings of the Buddha will help you to realise that truth and remember who you are. Reconnecting with your true nature will dissolve the fears that block your writing, as well as overcome the suffering inherent in having an ego.

You can explore these ideas further in the glossary.

Now let's look at how to work with the slogans on a practical level.

Chapter 3: How to Practice with the Slogans

If you want to write well it makes sense to train your mind. You wouldn't go for a run without warming up, and you wouldn't run a marathon without training first. Writing is the same. You can't expect your mind to work straight out of the box, as it were. So how do you go about training your mind?

First, you need to become aware of your mind and how it works from day to day. You function on autopilot much of the time, running unconscious programmes and automatic reactions. This is ideal territory for the ego to maintain its reign of control through fear. As we saw in Chapter One, the ego is a defensive structure that tries to keep you safe, but you often end up feeling disconnected from others and cut off from your own deeper Self.

The slogans disrupt the ego's habits and undermine its structures. They work against your tendency to control everything and make every situation and problem about 'me.' They wake you up and force you to pay attention to what you're doing and thinking about moment by moment.

Each slogan is a short, easily remembered phrase that you can use as the basis for meditation or contemplation. They're not meant to be taken as instructions on how to behave, as in the Ten Commandments or Buddhist precepts. They're not a stick to beat yourself with, but guidelines to be used with flexibility and commonsense.

All the slogans work together as a complete teaching, and you may notice some overlap between them. This is deliberate as it encourages you to approach the same problem from multiple angles. They're also often contradictory in order to provide balance and encourage you to really think about what you're doing so you don't go too far in one direction.

Although you don't need to be a Buddhist to benefit from using the slogans, the teachings provide an important context for understanding the ideas. While you can dip into the book in any order and use the slogans that resonate with you and your particular situation, I would recommend you start from the beginning for context first. Please don't be put off by the philosophy in the first few slogans! These provide the foundation for the rest of the slogans, so if you skip them you won't get the most out of the practice.

I'll do my best to explain and contextualise the slogans for you. I've been studying and practising Buddhism for twenty years so any mistakes or misperceptions are mine and subject to the limits of my understanding. I urge you to explore further using the resources in the appendix if you feel it would be of benefit.

The foundational teachings in lojong are quite advanced and challenging, so take your time with the early slogans to be sure you understand. It will help if you already have a meditation practice. If you don't, now is a good time to begin! You will find instructions for a basic meditation practice in Slogan 3.

Each slogan discusses the original teaching before going on to explore how you can apply it to your writing practice, and then finishes with some practical exercises so you can explore the teachings for yourself. How you do this is up to you. It might be a good idea to commit to a daily writing practice that incorporates the slogans, or perhaps you could integrate it into your existing routine. If you write a daily journal or do morning pages, you could pick a different slogan to explore each day, or set aside a special time to work with the slogans.

If you have a meditation practice, you could choose a slogan to contemplate, study the teaching and then sit for a time to meditate on what you have learned. After half an hour or so of contemplation, you could then write in a journal any insights that have come up.

You could also incorporate the slogans into a process of self-inquiry or therapy using free writing or journaling, or perhaps even use them as inspiration for crafted works, such as poems, short stories, novels, or non-fiction pieces like blog posts, articles or memoir.

To learn the slogans and internalise them, you might like to write them out on index cards or post-it notes. You could also spend time exploring the references and resources in the appendix, or use my slogan randomiser: **lojongforwriters.wordpress.com**

Sometimes a slogan immediately resonates with you and you know exactly how to apply it and what you need to learn from it. But others may take a little more thought and time. I don't want to give you too much direction because you will need to find your own way of working with them. This is about getting back in touch with your inner voice, so the process will be different for every individual. But here are a few suggestions:

Choose a slogan to work with over a period of a few days. You can do them in any order you like, but get familiar with the first ten slogans before you move on to the rest because these provide the foundation for the whole practice.

On day one, meditate on the slogan and reflect on its meaning

On day two, write about your experience with the slogan, explore its meaning, note any insights you gain, feelings that come up, and so on

On day three, choose another slogan and continue the pattern

Or you can work with each slogan over a longer period and apply them to various parts of your life, making notes in your journal as you go. For example:

- Day one: meditate on the slogan and its meaning
- Day two: apply the slogan to your spiritual practice
- Day three: apply it to your writing
- Day four: apply it to your relationships
- Day five: apply it to your family life
- Day six: apply it to your work
- Day seven: have a break!

You can do this however you like, and can even make up your own slogans. These can be based on the lojong slogans presented here, or you can create new ones that make sense to you and your situation. Keep them short and snappy, and make sure they're positive. You probably already have some favourite phrases that reflect your own hard won wisdom and insight, and even clichés can be helpful at the right time, such as: *"Let Go and Let God,"* "Count to Ten," or "It's All Good!"

After you've worked with these slogans for a while, they get into your subconscious and simmer away in the background. Then one day, when you're struggling with a problem and feeling stuck, a slogan will pop into your mind – like a reminder or an alarm going off – and prod you into realising where you've gone wrong. It's a bit like having an internal GPS system – Buddha GPS – that nudges you back onto your true path.

However you approach the slogans, may they be of benefit to you and your writing. May your pen and your mind be free!

Part Two

Mind Training
Slogans for Writers

~

Slogan 1: First, remember the basics

This slogan is about beginnings and the initial intention behind the act of starting something new. The original slogan is: *"First, train in the preliminaries,"* which refers to the basic facts of life, the things you can't avoid and which form the basis of all your actions. The four preliminaries are:

- Life
- Death
- Karma
- Suffering

These four are the foundation for the rest of this practice. Everything you do in your life falls within the bounds of these basic principles, and your attitude to each will determine how you live and the choices you make. Your feelings about life, death, karma, and suffering will influence all your actions, whether you are aware of it or not.

The first is your attitude to life itself. Life is precious and human life is incredibly rare, especially when you realise that there are billions more bacteria than there are human beings. The odds of you being born are vanishingly small. There are fewer atoms in the entire universe than there are chances of you coming into existence at all. So the fact that you exist is extraordinary. You are truly exceptional. Nobody like you has ever existed before and will never exist again.

In Buddhism, they talk of the preciousness of human life and how hard it is to attain. The odds of you being born is compared to the likelihood of a blind sea turtle coming to the surface of the ocean once every 100 years and managing to stick its head into a yoke that just happens to be floating there.

Second is your attitude towards death. This is the one thing that most people would rather not think about, but you know that death is certain. No matter what you do, you're never going to become immortal.

You might not like the idea of death, but it is essential to life. Death is part of the great cycle of change, and without it, nothing could live.

Coming to terms with your mortality is an important part of growing up and yet many people never really deal with the idea of death until it's staring them in the face. If you spend your life trying to avoid something that is unavoidable, this will have a profound effect on the choices you make. Death can happen at any moment and you have no idea when that might be. When you accept this truth, it provides the focus you need to make better choices.

Third are your feelings about karma. You don't have to believe in reincarnation to understand this; it is simply the chain of cause and effect that drives the cycle of change. Every action has a consequence and that means every moment in your life counts. Every thought you have and every action you take is meaningful because together they create an interconnected web that shapes your life.

However this also means you can't escape the consequences of your actions and your choices. There may be times when you would prefer to look the other way, but whether you try to do good or not, the laws of cause and effect will play themselves out in your life.

Finally, how you deal with suffering will shape your life and drive your choices. Buddhism describes suffering (*dukkha*) as a feeling of incompleteness or dissatisfaction, which is caused by the contraction against reality that creates the ego, as we saw in Chapter One. The ego retreats behind its defensive walls because the impermanence of life makes you feel insecure, but this also gives rise to suffering because you feel cut off from the flow of life.

You don't like the fact that everything changes. You don't like the fact that you will die and so will everybody you love. You don't like it when things go wrong, when you get ill, or old, or lose your job, or run out of ketchup and have to eat your burger dry. But that's life.

This slogan asks you to face up to reality and the basic facts of life. When you remember the basics it means taking responsibility for the fact that you are alive and being willing to deal with whatever comes your way. The quality of your life and happiness depend on how you approach these basic truths. You can't avoid your problems or wallow in your suffering.

The foundation for your life, and the rest of this practice, is to stand on your own two feet and say yes to embracing the life you have. This slogan encourages you to begin this practice with the intention to improve your life by taking responsibility for how you use your mind and the choices you make.

For Writers

There are various ways to apply this slogan to your writing. The basics could be the craft of writing, for example. Craft is an important foundation for your writing practice. The rules of grammar, spelling, and punctuation, are essential, and it never hurts to learn more about story structure and how to write prose, dialogue, and so on.

You could also think about how you begin writing, the process of sitting down and gathering your thoughts. How you begin any task, the state of mind you're in and how you feel about what you're doing, will lay the foundation for the work you do and inform how it turns out in the end.

But more basic than either of these is the intention behind your desire to write, and this is closest to the meaning of the original slogan. Intention is the foundation – it comes before you begin to write and before craft. You must have the intention to begin and the intention to improve your writing before you do anything else.

So this slogan reminds you to examine your intention: **Why do you write?**

The answer may be obvious or you may need to spend some time exploring your motivations. You may have many reasons for writing: to express yourself, to entertain others, to make money, explore ideas, impress somebody, or as personal therapy, and so on. Your reasons don't have to make sense to anybody else, they don't even have to make sense to you, and they can even be contradictory. Whatever your reasons, you need to understand and accept them.

For your writing to have the best possible foundation, it needs to be built on your most authentic truths. Your true voice can only come from the deepest part of yourself. This slogan is a reminder to come back to basics and remember why you're writing in the first place.

For example, if you keep worrying what others will think and it's blocking your writing, reconnecting with your original intention can help to reignite your self-belief and get your pen moving again. Or if you're struggling to motivate yourself and getting side-tracked by procrastination, or other responsibilities keep eating into your writing time, this slogan can give you a much needed kick.

To connect with your deepest intentions it can help to remember the four preliminaries – the basic facts of life – and apply them in your writing. This slogan reminds you to recognise the exceptional nature of your life. Your voice is unique and only you can find it and express it. Don't waste your time on activities that have no value to you. Your life is a one-off opportunity to be the best you that you can be. Nobody else can do it for you.

Begin well and the rest will fall into place.

Exercises

Begin a journal to track your progress through the slogans.

In your slogan journal, write about your intentions: Why do you write?

Based on your intentions, make a commitment to your writing and acknowledge its importance in your life. You might like to write your commitment as a promise to yourself and place it somewhere you can see it everyday.

Reflect upon the four preliminaries of the original slogan and write about what they mean to you:
- What is precious in your life?
- How do you feel about dying?
- Are you a force for good in your life?
- What causes you the most suffering?

Tell your unique story. Write about the key events, inner and outer, that have made you who you are, and make a commitment to move forward from now in a way that opens your life to more freedom and authenticity.

Slogan 2: See everything as a dream

This slogan is about seeing through the illusion of reality and going with the flow of life. It appears to contradict the previous slogan, which challenges you to accept the hard facts of life and deal with reality head on. Now you're asked to see reality as a dream, so are the facts of life real or not?

The original slogan is: "*Regard all dharmas as dreams,*" and it contradicts the previous slogan for a reason. Facing up to the facts of life and death is pretty heavy and you might be tempted to take yourself too seriously. So this slogan encourages you to lighten up and see everything as a dream.

Before we look at what that involves, we need to understand what the original slogan means by 'dharmas.' The word *dharma* has many meanings within different cultures. In Buddhism it has three:

- dharma, as in cosmic law and the natural order of life
- Dharma, as in the teachings of the Buddha
- and dharmas, as in phenomena

The slogan refers to the plural, dharmas, so it's talking about all the phenomena that make up your perception: what you're thinking, feeling, sensing, and so on. Your perception is constructed from multiple flashes of sense data, or phenomenon, that are constantly changing.

Reality is like this too. Everything is constantly changing and becoming something else. You can't pin anything down or control it. You can't get hold of reality and keep it still. It never stops moving, and your mind never stops moving either. The impermanent nature of reality tends to make you feel insecure so you resist the flow. But there's no need to react to this relentless churn with anxiety because underneath it all is the fact of absolute bodhicitta.

As we saw in Chapter Two, absolute bodhicitta is the true nature of reality. Everything that happens arises from this foundation of impermanence, which reveals that life is essentially illusory. That doesn't mean that reality doesn't exist. It means everything that exists – trees, dogs, thoughts, clouds, dreams – depends on other things for their existence. Nothing can exist separately from anything else because everything is interdependent.

This is described in Buddhism as *shunyata,* or emptiness. Everything that appears to exist arises due to causes and conditions – one thing leads to another, but nothing can appear on its own because nothing inherently exists. That doesn't mean reality isn't real. Emptiness isn't nothing, but 'no-thing.' In other words, there are no 'things' that exist separately. Not even you. (More on Emptiness in the glossary)

Arising from the foundation of pure awareness in absolute bodhicitta, you are interdependently interconnected to the whole of existence where everything is in a state of flux. You are part of that playful dream-like unfolding of reality and constantly in the process of becoming something new.

This slogan is encouraging you to let go and join the dance.

For Writers

This slogan reminds you of the importance of dreams and imagination. It's easy to become weighed down with the necessities of life and the drudgery of paying the bills. The great idea you had for a story gets pushed to the end of a long list of other responsibilities and forgotten. But this slogan says: dreams matter.

> *"The creative act expresses our inherent perfection and enlarges the universe by making visible the invisible."* – John Daido Loori

Imagination is just as important as the rest of your life. If everything is like a dream, then why shouldn't you follow the dreams of your soul and create something new.

Imagination is the essence of creativity but it must be cultivated. You need to create space in your life for your dreams and inspiration to take root and grow. This can be difficult when so many other demands crowd your time and headspace. Seeing everything as a dream can help you to let go and go with the flow of events.

That doesn't mean you should ignore important responsibilities and drift off into a dream world. It means remembering that everything is empty. Problems and stressful situations aren't as solid and unchanging as they appear, so if you're having a bad day, this slogan can act as a stress buster and remind you that this too shall pass.

When you're feeling uninspired and stuck with writer's block, or you want to write but don't know what to write about, open up to the flux of life and see what comes up. Go looking for connections. Invite inspiration in. Remember that everything is constantly becoming something else.

Your stuckness won't last so don't hold on to it.

Exercises

If you don't already have one, start a dream diary.

Take one of your dreams and turn it into a story.

In your slogan journal, explore how inspiration works. Where do your thoughts come from and where do they go? Where does your imagination come from? Where do story ideas come from?

What inspires you? Commit to spending more time doing the things you find inspiring.

Think of a new story idea – try to catch inspiration in the act.

Slogan 3: Examine the nature of awareness

This slogan is about exploring the nature of reality and your own mind. With the previous slogan you realised everything is like a dream. Now you turn your attention inwards to see who is watching this dream unfold. The original slogan is: *"Examine the nature of unborn awareness,"* in other words, what's going on behind all the noise in your mind.

The light of your conscious mind is so bright that it tends to drown out everything else. Your ego thinks it's running the show and takes up a lot of space; so much so that you think this is who you are. You may think, *"I am the person thinking. I am the person reading this. I am the person writing."* But if you look for that 'I', for the person behind the thought, what do you find?

When you turn your attention inwards and try to catch yourself seeing or thinking or feeling, a curious thing happens. You disappear. There is no one seeing or thinking or feeling – there is just the seen, the thought, the feeling. When you look for the person behind the experience – the experiencer – all you find is awareness.

Everything that you experience happens in your awareness. You don't tend to notice this space in which experience occurs because you're focused on the contents of the experience – the sensation, feeling, thought, and so on. The contents of awareness loom so large in your mind that you don't notice the awareness itself.

Most of the time you're hardly conscious that you're aware in the first place. You can get through whole days on autopilot without ever having a conscious thought. The process of being aware is something you take for granted, and if you're not aware of something then it's as if it never happened. But there are many things going on in your mind that never reach your conscious awareness because your brain filters them out.

For example, I've just eaten, so my stomach is busy digesting, but even if I concentrate really hard, I'm not aware of the acids and bile pouring into my guts. Which is probably a good thing. It's only when something goes wrong, that I become aware of certain bodily functions.

In fact, the majority of what happens in your body and mind is unconscious, and the most important thing to slip your attention is awareness itself. So this slogan asks you to pay attention to the process of being aware and become curious about how awareness works. If you do, you might discover something liberating about the nature of reality and the mind. (More on Awareness in glossary)

> *"What we call the mind is not really there at all. If it is truly something, it must have characteristics, such as colour... Or it must have shape like a pillar or a vase. It must be big or small, old or young, and so on. You can find out whether the mind exists or not by just turning inwards and reflecting carefully. You will see that the mind does not begin or end or stay anywhere; that it has no colour or form and is to be found neither inside nor outside the body. And when you see that it does not exist as any thing, you should stay in that experience without an attempt to label or define it."* – Dilgo Khyentse Rinpoche, *Enlightened Courage*

For Writers

When you're stuck and don't know what to write, it can feel as if you will never have another good idea ever again. You mind feels like a solid unmoving block. Every thought arrives stillborn, limp and lacking that essential spark. Self-doubt and negative thinking just make the situation worse.

By turning your attention inwards and noticing the awareness behind every thought and feeling, no matter how dark and dispiriting, you can begin to relieve the mental cramp caused by the ego and its fearful voice. It's a relief to discover that there's more space and life inside your head than you realised.

This slogan can help you to cut through distractions and noise by reminding you of the open space in which every thought arises.

Becoming more aware of your awareness will give you a short cut to an instant empty mind, and an open playground for your creativity to come to life.

When your environment is conspiring against you with endless distractions, or your mind is overflowing with too many thoughts all vying for your attention, it can be hard to concentrate. Instead of getting caught up in the noise and letting your mind become scattered, this slogan reminds you to take a step back. By focusing on your awareness, you can clear your head of clutter and open a space in which you can think more clearly.

Cultivate a regular meditation practice to train your mind to turn inwards towards your innate stillness. You can use your own method or follow the meditation guidelines below.

Exercises

Commit to a regular meditation practice using these guidelines:

- Sit on a cushion with your legs crossed, or on a hard-backed chair if your knees can't take sitting on the floor. Keep your back as straight as you can and relax your shoulders. Get the fidgets out of the way and settle into your seat.
- Breathe through your nose. Allow the breath to fill your abdomen but don't force it. Breathe naturally – no need to slow it down or try too hard.
- Just relax and breathe. Settle into a rhythm and become aware of your body sitting on the cushion or chair. Close your eyes or lower your gaze.
- If you like, you can count your breaths on the exhalation. Count to 10 and then start again. Or simply breathe and let everything go.
- If thoughts intrude bring your mind back to the breath. Don't give yourself a hard time for losing concentration. Simply return to the breath.
- Keep breathing, and stay centred in your body, for at least ten minutes.

- As you breathe, notice who is breathing. Can you find the self behind the breath?
- At the end of the session, bring your awareness back to the room.
- Slowly stand and return to your day. Bring with you the intention to stay focused and remember you can return to your breath anytime you feel the need.

Practice noticing your awareness of whatever you're doing, and try to catch yourself in the act. Pay attention and ask yourself: *Who is walking? Who is driving? Who is talking? Who is writing?*

Write in your journal and watch how the words come into your awareness as you write them down. See if you can catch yourself forming the words. Do you decide what to say, or do the words just appear?

Slogan 4: Don't hold on to your stories

This slogan is about letting go of your ideas about reality. The original slogan is: *"Self-liberate even the antidote,"* which is quite abstract so it will need some explanation. In simple terms, it means don't take the slogans too seriously. They are just ideas or thoughts in your mind. They may be useful tools, but it's important not to get too attached to them.

To put this into context we need to understand the nature of emptiness. The last couple of slogans have been pointing out that reality is dream-like and empty of inherent existence. Everything is interconnected and impermanent, so everything can only exist in relation to everything else. Nothing can exist by itself.

In Buddhism, this is called *shunyata*, or emptiness, and it means that everything is selfless, or empty of itself. To understand this is to self-liberate; in other words, to see through the nature of the self, to see that it is empty. The antidote is exactly that process of seeing through to emptiness. So this slogan is saying that even emptiness is empty. (More on Emptiness in glossary)

As Pema Chodron explains, *"Don't hold on to anything – even the realisation that there's nothing solid to hold on to."*

When you meditate regularly you can become attached to the idea of letting go of everything and going with the flow. You've seen that reality is like a dream and that even your sense of self is always changing. Underneath that is the open space of awareness and it can feel peaceful to relax into it and just be. After all the worrying and running around, it can be liberating to drop the anxiety and float off into emptiness.

But this is a trap. This slogan reminds you not to get attached to any particular way of seeing reality. Don't get caught up in being peaceful and letting go because it can cause problems. It can become a way to justify being lazy or not trying hard enough to change your circumstances or achieve something in the world. You can end up turning the idea of surrender into another identity to cling to, rather than recognising that there is no one who can surrender.

Any idea or belief system can be turned into a structure in your mind that your ego can use to either make itself seem larger and more powerful, or to hide behind because it feels weak and frightened. This slogan says there is no need to bolster your identity or hide from your fears – both are illusions and both are empty.

Whatever reality is, you're unlikely to ever understand it and you're certainly never going to be able to control it. Telling yourself stories and then clinging to them in the hope that, by doing that, you'll make them true, will never work. In the end, you can't let go of yourself because there is no self to let go of. When you understand that, you are free.

For Writers

Writing stories can help to liberate you from your own story because, once you've been writing for a while, you begin to see how easy it is to change a story. There are multiple ways to look at a particular event and every character in a story will see things differently. This forces you to detach from one viewpoint and explore alternative perspectives. If a story gets bogged down or goes wrong, it's not a problem because you can change it.

The story isn't fixed. You don't have to hold on to it.

You can apply this to your own life too. When you feel stuck, you can look at the stories you have been telling yourself and change them. Of course, it's not always that simple. First you have to discover what those stories are, and then you have to let them go.

You can dig those stories out by noticing the patterns that keep repeating in your life. Maybe the same problems come up all the time, or the same thoughts keep you awake every night. For example, pay attention to the beliefs that underpin your identity. Some of them may be helpful, but others could be causing you problems, such as:

"I'll never be successful."
"Nobody is interested in what I have to say."
"I don't have time to write."

Using this slogan, you can remind yourself that these are just ideas and you don't have to believe them. None of the stories in your mind have any inherent reality, they're all empty and impermanent. Whatever you believe about yourself, it's just a story and stories can be changed.

Another way to work with this slogan is to remind yourself that you don't always have to work in one particular way. If you write novels and believe you could never be a poet – why not? Perhaps the *"I'm not a poet"* story is one you no longer need to hold on to.

You might also believe you have to feel a certain way in order to write, or that you can only write under certain conditions – with a particular pen, for example, or only in a café, or only after you've done all your chores. You might not write unless you can achieve the 'right' state of mind: peaceful or clear or not confused or not scared. But if you keep waiting for the perfect conditions – either in life or in your mind – you'll never get any writing done. (See also Slogan 50)

Nothing in life is guaranteed. You never know what will happen next, so you have to write, regardless.

The hardest story for a writer to let go of is the idea of being a writer. Writing is hard work and there's no guarantee it will make you happy or rich or bring you peace. Whatever you think you want out of writing – let it go. That doesn't mean you stop writing, it just means: don't be attached to it.

Exercises

In your slogan journal, list all the stories you believe about who you are. How many of them are true?

Explore who you would be, or what you would do, if you didn't write.

Write your life story from the perspective of somebody else in your life, a sibling, partner, or parent. Or even better, a pet.

Take one moment from your past when you made a decision that sent you down a particular path and imagine what would have happened if you had made a different choice. Write the story of that parallel life.

Slogan 5: Rest in Beginner's Mind

This slogan is about resting in the awareness you discovered in Slogan 3, so if you don't already have a regular meditation practice, now would be a good time to begin.

The original slogan is: "*Rest in the nature of alaya, the essence.*" Alaya is the essence of consciousness, your sense of knowing or awareness. It is Buddha nature – empty and luminous with wisdom. So this slogan is about simply resting in your true nature, not looking into it and examining it, as you did in Slogan 3. Now you simply let it be.

A good foundational meditation practice is to sit and focus on your breathing; you can place your attention on a particular point in your body, if you like, such as your diaphragm rising and falling or the breath passing over your top lip. You don't have to try to do anything, just be with whatever is there. Don't try to stop your thoughts, just let them go. It might help to visualise your mind as a vast open sky and your thoughts as clouds drifting by or dissolving into nothing.

The essential nature of awareness is stillness and emptiness. This is the gap between thoughts, the space in which everything is held. Noticing these gaps, or pauses, can help you become more aware of the stillness that underpins all of your experience. The more you practice meditation, the clearer your mind will become and it should become easier to rest in the spaciousness of awareness.

When you rest in the mind you're not disappearing into your head or floating away from the world. Awareness isn't separate from experience; it is the ground from which experience arises. It isn't rooted in the head, but in the heart. While the heart knows reality directly, the head can only reflect reality through thought. This is why bodhicitta means 'awakened heart and mind' to distinguish it from the intellect.

The mind is grounded in the body and this is the medium through which you experience life. So if you catch yourself spacing out during meditation, bring your attention back to the breath. This will help to keep you rooted in your body and stop the mind from drifting.

The real challenge of meditation isn't to stop your mind running away with the faeries, but to get it to shut up in the first place. Even when you're relaxed, the mind continues to burble away to itself. Sometimes, when you begin to meditate, the noise in the mind appears to get worse. But why does it do this?

The mind keeps moving because it wants to understand and control reality. This is impossible, but your mind keeps trying anyway. The incessant churn is a defence against silence. The mind can't stop thinking because if it did, it would drop into stillness and emptiness, and that would reveal the truth – that you don't know anything and you're not in control.

The mind runs away from the silence, from not knowing, but that's like trying to run away from your own legs. Stillness, and silence, is where the mind comes from. You can't get away from it because it's who you are. So this slogan asks you to embrace not knowing and rest in the open spaciousness of your true nature.

For Writers

Meditating before you begin to write is an excellent way to clear your mind of unwanted and distracting thoughts. But it can be hard to convince yourself to sit and do nothing, even for just ten minutes a day.

Finding the time to write is a challenge in itself. You may be exhausted from running around, desperate for a break but too busy to stop. You feel under pressure to be productive and feel guilty doing nothing. Even on holiday you feel duty-bound to see as many sights as possible, stockpile experiences, take photos, shoot videos, tweet your lunch. You can't just sit and be.

You may believe there's nothing to be gained from being still, but it's only when you finally stop that you realise how much tension you're carrying in your body. Your breathing is shallow and your shoulders are scrunched up to your ears. When you write in this state, the results are often disappointing.

So when you feel stuck or you're struggling to find the right words, take a moment to stop and notice what is going on in your body. Take a few deep breaths. Close your eyes and just feel where you are.

To do your best writing you need to allow yourself to rest. This slogan is urging you to stop and simply be with what is present in your life. Stop running around and smell the roses. If you take the time to do this every day, your mind will begin to settle and you will come to a place of deep rest and inner peace.

This slogan also reminds you that to create anything you must embrace not knowing. If you approach your writing with the assumption that you know what you're doing, you'll fall into old habits and patterns. Your work will become predictable and unimaginative. As Shunryu Suzuki says, "*In the beginner's mind there are many possibilities, in the expert's mind few.*" (See also Slogan 30)

To create anything you must take a leap into the unknown and this can trigger fears and anxieties. Your mind reacts to the uncertainty by over-thinking and trying to control your experience. But this is a fool's errand. You will never find your voice by listening to the machinations of the intellect.

Your true voice comes from the heart and this can be found by resting in the awareness and unknowing of your beginner's mind.

Exercises

Incorporate meditation into your daily writing practice. Before you begin to write, sit for at least ten minutes and watch your breath. Don't try to stop yourself thinking, but imagine your mind as a huge open space, like the sky or outer space. Breathe into this space and relax.

In your slogan journal, free write for ten minutes about all the things you don't know. You can complete these sentences to get you started:
- I know nothing about...
- I will never understand...
- I don't know why...

Embrace the unknown by writing in a medium you've never tried before. If you're a novelist write a poem, if you write short stories begin a novel, and so on.

Slogan 6: Play in the dream

This slogan is about applying everything you have learned in the previous slogans to your daily life. Mind training isn't just about meditation. You have to put it to practical use to make life better for yourself and others.

The original slogan is: *"In post-meditation, be a child of illusion."* Although this seems to be referring to what happens after you finish meditating, in reality, you can't separate meditation from post-meditation. Life isn't divided into separate sections and you can't say that one part of your life is spiritual while another part isn't. What you do when you meditate affects your whole life.

So this slogan encourages you to remember the feeling of openness and space that you experience while meditating, as you go about your day. You can practice this all the time by being mindful of your thoughts and reactions. Pay attention to whatever you experience without getting caught up in the stories you tell yourself about what is happening. Simply focus on what's in front of you.

Mindfulness can liberate you from negative thought patterns and behaviour, but this slogan contains a subtle warning. There's a danger that if you apply your spiritual practice to every aspect of your life, you could become too serious. You might start to believe you always have to be good and nice and pious. You might pride yourself on how calm and mindful you are, and become too precious about maintaining your spiritual poise.

This slogan tells you not to take yourself so seriously, but to play like a child. The beginner's mind of the previous slogan reminds you that you don't really know anything, not for certain. A beginner's mind is like the mind of a child: open and curious about life, full of joyful enthusiasm and spontaneity. So this is how you are to approach your spiritual practice and your life.

You can't control reality because it's constantly changing and inherently mysterious and uncertain. You know that if you try to control your experience it leads to suffering. So the only sane response, if you want to stop suffering, is to let go and play in the illusion.

Slogan 2 encouraged you to see everything as a dream, and the best you can do with a dream is to play and have some fun with it. Who knows what will happen next?

For Writers

This slogan is useful to remember when you can't stop worrying about some future possibility or problem. Every time you sit down to write, you begin to think about what will happen if nobody likes what you're writing, or whether anyone will publish your book, or if they will even want to read it in the first place.

With your beginner's mind you know that you don't know what will happen and there's no way you can know. So this slogan tells you to lighten up and stop worrying about things you can't control, and have some fun.

Write your book because you want to write it. Write your stories because you enjoy the process of discovering who these characters are. It's fun to throw two mismatched people into a situation and watch how they work things out. As a writer you get to play in the dream every time you sit down to write. Don't spoil your own fun by taking yourself or the writing so seriously that you can't enjoy it.

This slogan can also be helpful when you feel yourself getting too rigid in your approach, especially in the early stages of a project. When you're writing the first draft of a novel, for example, there's no need to get hung up on the correct spelling, punctuation, and grammar. At this stage it's more important to get the words out of your head and onto the page without that pesky inner critic getting in the way. This is sometimes called the 'vomit draft' – you just spew your brains onto the page!

For many writers, this is the best part of the process, when you get to explore, experiment, and surprise yourself. But if you find yourself doubting every other word, or going over and over the same passages, tweaking and making changes – stop. Remind yourself to play in the dream. You can edit later.

Free writing is an excellent way to practice playing in the dream. The technique can be used before you start your 'proper' writing as a way to limber up and get your pen moving. There are no real rules for free writing, the idea is to simply write and not censor yourself. You can choose a topic to write about or literally write whatever comes into your head.

Free writing is just for you, nobody else needs to read it, so don't hold back – write whatever needs to come up. You can do it however you like or follow these guidelines, adapted from *Writing Down the Bones* by Natalie Goldberg:

- Set a time limit, from 10 to 30 minutes.
- Keep your hand moving – don't stop to read what you've written or edit or cross things out, even if you make a 'mistake.'
- Don't worry about spelling, punctuation or grammar, and don't even worry about making sense. If you make a mistake, just keep going.
- Don't think or analyse. Just write.
- If you go blank, write about what you're feeling, or describe what's right in front of you.
- If you feel resistance or boredom, write about that and explore why.
- When the time is up, look at what you have and keep any interesting phrases or ideas to use later if you want.

Exercises

If you don't already do it, incorporate a short session of free writing into your daily writing practice. Spend at least ten minutes writing waffle before you begin to write 'for real.'

Give yourself permission to write badly. You can do this every time you sit down to write, or try the following exercise.

Write like a child – get some crayons, felt tip pens or coloured pencils and write a story as if you were child. Don't worry if the story makes no sense – go wild! Write in exercise books or on plain paper so you don't have to worry about writing neatly. You may also like to sit on the floor or at a low table to get in the mood.

Illustrate your story – draw some illustrations for the story you have just written, or for a story you already have. You don't have to be an artist or have any talent – just have some fun.

Slogan 7: Practice Sending and Receiving

This slogan introduces the meditation practice of tonglen where you're encouraged to move towards pain and suffering with an open and compassionate heart in order to heal.

The original slogan is: "*Sending and taking should be practised alternately. These two should ride the breath.*" Sending and taking is also known as sending and receiving, and refers to the practice of tonglen. This is a meditation practice where you breathe in (receive) difficulty and suffering, and breathe out (send) compassion.

Tonglen may seem counterintuitive because it's the opposite of what you would normally do. Usually you try to avoid feeling pain or doing things that make you uncomfortable. But this slogan asks you to move towards those things and embrace them instead.

Tonglen is practised for your own pain and suffering, as well as on behalf of others and it challenges you to widen the circle of your compassion as far as you can. It's easy to send love and healing to people you already care about, but why limit your compassion to those closest to you? You can't be truly loving and compassionate if there are some people you exclude from your circle of care. So tonglen is practised for everyone: people you love, people you dislike, people who have annoyed or hurt you in some way, and even people you hate.

When faced with a painful experience your instinct is often to shut down and close your heart. You turn away from pain in the hope that it will go away if you ignore it. But it doesn't go away. The pain will hide in the shadows of your unconscious, silently dictating your behaviour and slowly draining your life of joy and love.

You can't really love or live life to the full if you're not willing to feel pain and suffering because both are unavoidable. And feeling the pain of others is difficult to do if you can't feel your own. Tonglen helps you to get back in touch with all your painful feelings, whether these come from your own experience or from seeing others suffer and being unable to help.

Practising tonglen helps to keep your heart open to whatever you experience rather than shutting down and turning away. When you do this, it reveals that your pain is the same as others' pain. We all suffer in the same way and seeing this can help to dissolve the boundaries between yourself and others.

Suffering is universal and is caused by the denial of your true nature, so tonglen begins by dissolving the ego into the emptiness of bodhicitta. This open space in your heart is the source of compassion and your true Self. When you breathe suffering into your true nature, compassion naturally flows out in response.

For Writers

At first glance it might seem that tonglen has nothing to do with writing. But this practice contains the essence of the process of freeing your mind.

It's hard to write well when you don't trust yourself or even like yourself very much. When there are powerful negative emotions blocking your expression from the unconscious, it's going to take something equally powerful to shift them. Tonglen is the answer.

Your writing will be deeper, more honest, and more powerful, if you can go towards your pain rather than being scared of it. The practice of tonglen can help to dissolve fears and blockages that stop you writing the way you would like, and smooth over problematic relationships that cause difficulties in your writing career.

For example, if you're struggling to get your writing recognised by the publishing industry and the endless rejections are getting you down, rather than seeing agents and editors as the enemy, you could practice tonglen with them in mind. Dissolve your fears and anger against the industry that seems to be blocking your ambitions, and you may find a new perspective opening up.

It's doubtful that practising in this way would turn your luck around and bring a flood of appreciation your way, but you might begin to enjoy your writing again, regardless what anybody else thinks of it.

To practice tonglen, follow the instructions in the exercise.

Exercises

There's only one exercise for this slogan: the instructions for practising tonglen. Start practising for yourself by working with your own pain and suffering, then you can extend the practice to others.

Begin by meditating in the usual way. Sit until your mind settles into stillness and you feel calm.

When you're ready, drop all your attachments. Let go into stillness and allow the open spaciousness of bodhicitta to dissolve everything else. If it helps, you can visualise your mind as the sky or outer space.

Now breathe in the suffering, the heavy dark feeling, and breathe out peace and spaciousness. When you breathe in, you're taking the suffering into the open space at the centre of your heart – imagine the pain dissolving into the open sky as you breathe in. This way, the pain doesn't get stuck because you're not holding onto it. Visualise it in any way that makes sense to you and makes it easier to do the mediation.

Continue to breathe in darkness, restriction, frustration, contraction, heaviness, tension, stress, irritation (anger, fear, grief, and so on), and breathe out relaxation, spaciousness, peace, letting go, lightness, compassion, surrender.

It may take a little while to transform some of the darker feelings because of the defences you've built up over the years. Just keep practising and they will slowly dissolve.

When you feel ready, you can continue the practice for somebody else. Choose a particular person or situation and feel their pain and suffering, and breathe out compassion. Practice first with somebody you love and feel close to. Then you can practice with somebody you have problems with, and finally you can practice with an enemy or someone you have real difficulty accepting.

Sometimes the compassion feels blocked and you can't do the practice because there are too many feelings of resentment or irritation. If this happens, just work with whatever feelings are present. So breathe in your resentment and breathe out acceptance and compassion.

Slogan 8: Your problems are your gifts

This slogan is about working with your problems rather than trying to get rid of them or avoid them. It builds on the previous slogan and the practice of tonglen in order to transform suffering into happiness.

The original slogan is: "*Three objects, three poisons, and three seeds of virtue*," which needs some explanation. In simple terms, the three objects are the way you tend to either like, dislike, or feel neutral about things. The three poisons are the way you react to those objects with desire, aversion, or indifference. So if you like something you tend to desire it, if you dislike something you'll try to avoid it, and if you feel neutral you don't really care either way.

By reacting to things the way you do, you create your own suffering, which is why they're called poisons. Chasing after things you like or avoiding things you don't like only leads to pain in the end. So this slogan encourages you to accept things as they are instead, and this transforms the poisons into seeds of virtue.

In other words, your problems become your gifts. Or as Shunryu Suzuki puts it, "*For Zen students, a weed is a treasure.*"

This slogan is about how you label your experience of the world and your own feelings and thoughts. You tend to categorise everything that happens and then judge whether you like it, or not, and put it in a box in your head. These objects are classed as friends, enemies, or neutral, depending on how you feel about them, and they relate to both inner and outer experiences. So an object can be a particular feeling or thought, as well as people or situations in the world.

This tendency to categorise objects isn't necessarily a bad thing. There are situations you would be well advised to avoid: a speeding car, a hungry tiger, an untrustworthy person, and so on. But sometimes your judgements about people or situations can be way off base because they're coloured by unconscious assumptions, prejudices and fears.

When this happens you expect the world to conform to the labels in your head and that never ends well.

The poisons are what come up as a result of your reaction to the object. However, you're not really reacting to the object itself, but to the label you've attached to it. It's not the person or situation that's causing the problem, but the idea in your head that says, "*This is bad!*" or "*This is great!*" or "*I don't care about that.*"

There's nothing abnormal about this, it's just how your mind works from day to day. You want to feel good and don't want to suffer, so you tend to move towards things you think you'll enjoy and avoid the things you don't like. Everybody wants to feel happy and avoid pain and unhappiness, but you end up driven round and round by desire and aversion trying to fit reality into the neat little boxes in your head. This habitual reaction causes suffering because everything is constantly changing. You can't keep hold of the things you desire, and you can't completely get rid of the things you don't want.

This slogan says there's another way to look at the situation: the poisons can become seeds of virtue or goodness if you look at them the right way. Since you can't get rid of your suffering by ignoring it, you can turn towards it and transform it. When you accept things as they are and learn to live and let live, your suffering can be transformed into wisdom and compassion. The poison implodes in on itself and disappears, becoming the seed of virtue, which is simply seeing reality as it is.

For Writers

Writers often struggle with crippling levels of self-doubt, and that's true even on a good day when the writing is going well. You can't write without judging your work, taking it apart and figuring out how it can be improved. And this is before you even share your work with readers, who will have their own judgements to make. A certain amount of critical thinking is necessary and important, but if your inner critic gets the upper hand, you may find it almost impossible to write anything at all.

This slogan reminds you to notice your reactions and the patterns of thought that cause problems when you're writing. When you have a strong reaction, either positive or negative, step back and ask yourself what is really going on. What are you reacting to? Are you giving yourself a hard time because you think you're not writing well enough? Are you letting yourself off the hook, thinking you are writing brilliantly, when in fact you could do with rewriting the draft one more time?

Seeing your problems as gifts also encourages you to accept yourself as you are, and to work with what life has given you without trying to change it. Not all problems can be solved and you can't always overcome the difficulties with which you are faced. Sometimes you have to accept that a situation won't be transformed easily and perhaps the only thing you can do is learn to live with it.

This doesn't mean you have to give up on your dreams to write. You can take your stuck feelings, the stuff that just doesn't get better no matter how much you try, and lean into it. Stop trying to get away from it and let it be. Accept it as it is. Perhaps you can transform your reaction to the problem by turning the poison into something good – like a poem or a story.

Exercises

When you have a strong reaction to a person, situation, feeling or thought, stop and pay attention. Look into what just happened and see if you can find the source of your reaction. What judgement did you make?

Catalogue your reactions in your journal. Do you notice any patterns?

Think of a time in your life when you had an extreme reaction to something or someone that had serious consequences – good or bad. What would have happened if you had reacted differently? Write about it in your journal or fictionalise it in a story.

Take the story you have just written and change the reaction of one of the characters.

Slogan 9: Always train with the slogans

This slogan encourages you to apply the practice of mind training to everything in your life. The original slogan is: "*In all activities, train with slogans.*" Mind training isn't just about meditation and the slogans can be applied to pretty much anything. In fact, it was this slogan that gave me the idea for this book.

There are no experiences in your life that aren't coloured by what's going on in your mind. So the more you do to transform your mind, the more your life will change. Even if you only apply the slogans to training your mind, the effect will ripple out into the rest of your life.

Another way of looking at this is that there's no excuse for not meditating because you can do it anywhere and in all situations.

When you work with the slogans over time they tend to spontaneously appear in your mind as guidance whenever you need them. Once you have learnt them all and internalised them, your deeper Self will always know the best slogan for the occasion. The right slogan will pop into your mind just as you reach for another cookie, or lose your temper, or feel like giving up on your dreams.

You can adapt the slogans to suit yourself too, as I've done with some of the slogans here, or even make up your own. Favourites of mine include: "*Let it go!*" and "*Stop telling yourself stories!*" – which is similar to Slogan 4.

Working with the slogans helps to shift your attention away from indulging in your own problems or getting hung up on where you're stuck or unhappy, and towards a more open state of mind. They are designed to undermine the ego and its fears and this isn't an easy process. But the slogans help by giving you a structure to work with and a way to shift your perspective. You can stop obsessing about problems and instead begin to solve them, or even see that your problems aren't so bad after all.

The slogans wake you up to the present moment and help you to realise what you are doing, or not doing. They can jolt you out of your complacency or boredom or even depression. Wherever you feel stuck is where you can apply the slogans. They work like a reality check with a sense of humour, or a helpful friend who calls just at the right moment and says, *"Are you sure that's what you want to do?"*

For Writers

This slogan captures the essence of this book: rather than fight your mind and struggle with unconscious emotional difficulties that hold you back, you can find a way to work with your mind to transform it and set it free. You don't have to be at the mercy of your negative thinking or self-doubt. You can use the slogans to short-circuit your thought process and change your mind.

This slogan reminds you to keep working at this practice. Don't let the weakest part of yourself – your ego and its fears – spoil your enjoyment of life and prevent you from realising your dreams. If you want to write but find yourself stuck or going round in circles because of fears you can't control, this slogan says:

You *can* change your mind. It's just going to take some work.

If you haven't already done so, get some index cards and write one slogan on each. You can illustrate the cards, if you like, with anything that helps you to remember the meaning of the slogan. Shuffle the cards and keep them on the desk where you write. When you get stuck, pick a card out of the pile and then meditate on the slogan.

Or you can visit my slogan randomiser, **Lojong for Writers**, and pick a slogan from there. On the randomiser, each slogan includes a brief description of its meaning to help you understand how to work with it.

If you need a slogan to help with a specific problem, then the only way is to memorise the slogans and rely on your subconscious to do the heavy lifting. Don't worry, that is what it's good at! Work your way through this book and keep it close at hand. You may also like to explore some of the resources in the appendix to further your studies.

Exercises

Pick a slogan and work with it for a week. Meditate on it. Write about it.

Keep doing that until you have covered all 59 slogans.

Slogan 10: Practice self-acceptance

This slogan is about the tonglen meditation that was introduced in Slogan 7, and encourages you to begin the practice with yourself. The original slogan is: *"Begin the sequence of sending and taking with yourself,"* which is another way of saying practice self-acceptance.

Tonglen is about making friends with yourself and transforming your suffering with compassion. It's practiced on behalf of others, but it's hard to have compassion for others if you don't have it for yourself. So this slogan encourages you to heal your own pain first. Compassion really does begin at home.

To practice self-acceptance you need to be honest with yourself about what you're really feeling. You may avoid dealing with your suffering because it's painful, and distract yourself with busyness. You might even lie to yourself that everything is fine. You may believe you have no right to suffer because there are other people who are worse off than you, so you bury your true feelings deep inside.

First you need to acknowledge what you're really feeling and turn towards it with compassion. The pain you're feeling could be physical, but that's harder to deny, so here we're mostly talking about emotional and psychological pain in the form of suffering. For example, emotional wounds that won't heal, patterns of self-sabotage and low self-esteem, not being true to yourself, withholding love from yourself as well as others, feelings of inadequacy and shame, anxiety, fear, guilt, frustration, confusion, depression, rage, and despair. The list goes on and on.

The more you deny or repress or run away from your true feelings, the worse you will feel and the tighter your heart will become. You end up trapped inside your own pain and suffering, even if everything seems fine on the surface. When you avoid feeling the truth inside, it makes it harder to relax and enjoy life. So tonglen encourages you to say yes to your experience, no matter how painful it might be. It's about staying present with yourself and supporting yourself, even when you are struggling, rather than shutting down your heart.

By training yourself to turn towards your pain and suffering, you can transform difficult emotions into wisdom and happiness. In that way, pain becomes its own antidote, one that you can share with others.

> *"What you do for yourself – any gesture of kindness, any gesture of gentleness, any gesture of honesty and clear seeing toward yourself – will affect how you experience your world. In fact, it will transform how you experience the world. What you do for yourself, you're doing for others, and what you do for others, you're doing for yourself. When you exchange yourself for others in the practice of tonglen, it becomes increasingly uncertain what is out there and what is in here."*
> – Pema Chodron, *Start Where You Are*

For Writers

It's natural to want to improve yourself and your life. But the danger is that the more you try to make yourself better, the worse you feel. As a writer you want to improve your writing and make it as good as you can. You want to get rid of the things you don't like and become a better version of yourself. Perhaps you would like to be more popular, more productive, talented, and rich!

But every time you think you're not good enough at something, you are judging yourself and feeding the fears and self-doubt that make it so hard to write well.

This slogan encourages you to practice self-acceptance. Tonglen reverses your normal way of looking at yourself and asks you to embrace all the things you usually reject and push away. You will never become a better version of yourself by beating yourself up.

So whenever you feel stuck or scared or just a little doubtful of the way forward, turn towards that feeling instead of pushing it back into the darkness. As you make friends with yourself, you will find it easier to hear and express your true voice as a writer. Not only that, but embracing the full gamut of your emotions will also help you to write deeper and more believable characters.

The best characters in stories are the ones who are multidimensional. They have hidden depths and contradictions, strengths and weaknesses. It's the flaws and emotional blind spots in a character that drive the story, leading to wrong turns and mistakes that make for great conflict and drama. Conflict isn't something you tend to enjoy in real life, but in storytelling it's essential. So turning towards your dark side rather than denying it will help to give your characters more depth.

Practising tonglen and self-acceptance will also help you to make a deeper connection with your readers. Compassion comes from seeing the underlying unity of all life. Everybody and everything is interconnected. We all have the same problems and the same feelings. By tapping into your real human dilemmas and suffering, and finding a way to resolve your pain, you will be able to transform your writing into a something that can heal others because they recognise themselves in your work.

Exercises

In your slogan journal, write about where you feel stuck and the feelings that are holding you back.

Practice tonglen with those feelings until they start to transform. Refer to Slogan 7 for the instructions, and remember to breathe the difficult feelings into the open space of your heart and then let them go.

Identify a part of yourself that you have problems with – a fear, an embarrassing secret, or a failure – and create a character who embodies that trait. Write a story featuring this character as a hero or heroine and explore how the trait could be helpful.

Slogan 11: Turn obstacles into the Path

This slogan is about working with whatever happens, no matter how bad, rather than waiting for life to be perfect. The original slogan is: *"When the world is filled with evil, transform all mishaps into the path of bodhi."* The word *bodhi* means enlightenment, so this is saying that when things get difficult you can still practice meditation.

When life goes wrong and you don't get what you want, it triggers your ego to react in predictable, but negative ways. Maybe you get angry, or sulk, or look for somebody to blame. Perhaps you try to force life to do your bidding, cajoling and bullying people and circumstances to give you what you want. Or maybe, if things are bad enough, you give up altogether – what's the point in trying to make life better if it will just go wrong again?

You can't bludgeon obstacles into submission and you can't hide from life when it goes wrong; you have to use your intelligence. Try to understand the nature of the obstacle – is it a real problem, or is your attitude towards the situation causing most of the difficulty? This slogan reminds you that no matter what happens, you can choose to learn from it and take a more constructive approach that is open to the possibility of change.

You will never be able to force life to conform to your wishes and it will never be a perfect world. Change and improvement are possible, but life will never work exactly the way you want. Even if it does, it won't stay that way for long. You have to work with life as it is, which is pretty messy and complicated. It may not be perfect, but it can be good enough – for now.

You can't control reality or stop problems from occurring. The general ups and downs of life will happen no matter what you do, even if you try your best. So when you're confronted by a problem or obstacle, ask yourself if there's something you can do about it, and if there is, find a way to make it happen. If there's nothing you can do, you will have to accept the situation as it is.

Accepting things as they are doesn't mean you just give in to your problems or allow others to abuse or exploit you. It means you have the option of taking even the worst circumstances and using them to strengthen yourself by building resilience and wisdom in the face of suffering. You always have a choice.

This slogan reminds you to work with whatever comes up rather than reacting automatically and unconsciously to mishaps. Things don't always go the way you want but if you only meditate or practice mind training when you feel good and things are going well, you'll get stuck when you have a bad day.

The good news is that you don't have to wait for life to be perfect. If you can approach everything – good and bad – with mindfulness, then the obstacles in your life can become stepping-stones on the path to enlightenment.

In other words: when life gives you lemons, make lemonade!

For Writers

Life is impossible to control and there will always be times when things just don't go your way. You may grumble and gripe, but this does nothing to change the situation. But it can be too easy to use the problems in your life as excuses to avoid writing. Perhaps you say things like, *"I can't write now, I'm too distracted,"* or *"I can't write because I'm too angry about what the government are doing,"* or maybe you're too confused, or scared, and so on. But if you use every mishap in your life as an excuse not to write, you'll never get anything done. Every day will bring another problem and another day will go by without you having written a word.

When you try to create the perfect environment in which to write you spend more time fighting against reality than writing. You may be able to switch off your phone and avoid going online, but other distractions will be harder to control. So you'll need a different approach.

This slogan encourages you to work with the obstacles on your path rather than fighting them. Don't wait for the perfect moment – write anyway.

The difficult times in your life can become your most productive if you approach them the right way. When things get hectic and you have a million things to do, it forces you to get organised, so when you sit down to write you feel more single-minded. It forces you to concentrate and focus your energies on the things that matter. You're less likely to waste time on distractions because you're just too busy.

When life goes wrong, it reminds you of your priorities and how important writing is to your wellbeing. This can make you even more determined to write, despite the disaster unfolding in the rest of your life. Writing can also provide an escape from your problems, a way to recuperate and heal, and process your feelings in order to reach a deeper understanding of the situation.

Many of the obstacles you face will be internal rather than external. You can be distracted by your own doubts and fears, or by the reaction you have to your writing being rejected, for example. You may become discouraged or disillusioned because your story hasn't turned out the way you had hoped, or perhaps other people didn't enjoy it.

Everybody experiences rejection and criticism, but the important thing is to not become blocked as a result. Working with this slogan encourages you to become less reactive and more compassionate towards yourself and others. When others reject your work you can see it as an opportunity to learn and discover how you can improve your writing. Every rejection and criticism then becomes a step along the path to you becoming a better writer and the obstacles on your path will no longer stop you from writing.

Exercises

In your slogan journal, describe your perfect writing day. What would you have to change in order to create the perfect moment in which to write?

Write about the obstacles you face in your journal. These can be external distractions and problems in your life, or internal fears and doubts that get in the way of your writing.

Examine the obstacles you have written about and see if you can turn towards them with compassion. What can you learn from the obstacles you face? What opportunities do they contain? Write about how you can transform your obstacles in your journal.

Slogan 12: Take responsibility

This slogan is about breaking the cycle of blame that you get sucked into when things don't go the way you hope. The original slogan is: *"Drive all blames into one,"* which means instead of looking for somebody else to blame, you turn it around and take it on yourself. You are responsible.

That doesn't mean you have to blame yourself or make yourself feel guilty for everything. It's not about beating yourself up and thinking, *"It's all my fault!"* This slogan is just asking you to notice how often you try to avoid responsibility and to turn it around and think about what is really going on.

When things go wrong, watch the way you react. You might start by asking why the situation has happened, but then slip into looking for somebody else to blame. When something goes wrong, the question is always there in the back of your mind: *"Whose fault is it?"*

It's easy to do this, and it's usually automatic. You don't even think about it, and may even blame things that nobody has any control over, like the weather. For example, perhaps you decide to start a new exercise regime and plan to go for a run first thing in the morning. But when you get up and discover that it's raining, you end up not going. And then you blame the rain! *"I can't go for a run – it's raining."*

The rain is just an excuse, a way for you to pretend to yourself, and perhaps to others, that you're not being lazy. When you blame others, you tend to miss the part you have played in the conflict or problem that has arisen. So this slogan asks you to take responsibility for your choices and your reactions.

Blaming others doesn't change things or help to solve your problems. Being self-righteous doesn't help either. In fact, nobody can make you feel or do something that you don't accept on some level. So when you react to a problem by seeking to blame somebody else, it's probably because, deep down, you know you may be partly responsible for what has happened.

Obviously this isn't always the case. You may be the innocent victim of another's unscrupulous act, but you are still responsible for how you react. Regardless of what happens in any situation, only you have the power to change your own mind. And you do that by accepting responsibility for how you think and what you feel.

So this slogan encourages you to accept reality and pay attention to how you really feel about what happens. Don't try to dodge responsibility for your reactions. Be honest with yourself. Accept reality as it is, and then you can decide how to respond.

For Writers

This slogan encourages you to take responsibility for your writing and the choices you make. You can't blame others when they don't respond to your work the way you would like them to. For example, when your work is rejected, don't blame the agent or editor in question. There could be any number of reasons why they have rejected your writing. Check your work, improve it if necessary, and then send it out again to somebody else.

The same approach applies to dealing with reviews or criticism of your writing. When you receive a bad review, don't blame the other person and bitch to yourself about the idiot who clearly doesn't understand what you're trying to do. Look at your writing and ask yourself whether the criticisms are valid. If they are, make the necessary changes. However, if the criticisms are not valid – let them go.

Other people are allowed to not like your writing, and you are allowed to not like their criticism, but you are responsible for how you feel about their opinion. In the end, unless you have asked for feedback and you are genuinely trying to improve your writing, it is none of your business what anybody else thinks of your work.

If you don't write on a particular day, you can't blame anybody else. Even if others appear to be obstructing you and causing problems, you can choose to deal with that situation appropriately, and write anyway. You are the one who has to decide to write and then find the time to sit down and do the work. Nobody is standing over you with a big stick making you do it.

Only you can take responsibility for your writing. You may try to talk yourself out of it and come up with endless reasons why you can't do it, but in the end, you only have yourself to blame if you don't write. Perhaps if anybody can stop you from writing, then you're not a writer. That may sound harsh, but if you really want to write you will find a way to do it, no matter what your circumstances and no matter who appears to stand in your way.

Take responsibility for your dream of being a writer and make it happen. Write!

Exercises

On the days you don't write, who do you blame for your failure? Rant in your journal about all the people and circumstances that you have blamed. Hold nothing back, get it all out of your system.

On another day, re-read your Blame Rant and consider it dispassionately. If you were a character in a story, how would you feel about this person's behaviour? Are they whining, self-pitying or self-righteous? Can you feel compassion for this behaviour?

Write a story in which your Blame Rant character learns to change their ways and take responsibility. How does his or her behaviour change?

Slogan 13: Be grateful to everyone

This slogan, which is the same as the original, is about recognising that you are dependent upon everybody else for your existence. That might not be an easy idea to accept, especially when you have to deal with someone or something you don't like. But mind training is about befriending those parts of yourself, and others, that you reject.

Everybody has a shadow that contains all the qualities and characteristics that they don't like. As we saw in Chapter One, the shadow is created by the ego when it banishes the miscreants into the basement of the subconscious. But these rejected parts don't disappear once they are hidden in the darkness. The shadow contains a lot of potential energy and it's impossible to keep it in check, so it tends to spill out into the world.

You experience this as projection. In other words, you see in others the qualities and characteristics that you don't like in yourself. You even project positive qualities too, but it's the negative ones that cause most problems. Because the whole process happens subconsciously, you don't usually realise what you're doing. But you can rediscover the parts of yourself that you dislike by noticing how you react towards others. What you reject in others is a sign of something within yourself that could use a little acceptance and compassion.

Every time you have a strong reaction to somebody it provides an opportunity to practice acceptance. If you always react the same way, then you know there is something lurking in the basement that needs attention. And this works with positive reactions too. The people that inspire you, the people you admire, may reveal potentials you possess in yourself that you struggle to believe in.

Whether good or bad, the people and things you react strongly to, are reflections of your own being. So anybody can hold up a mirror that helps you to see yourself more clearly. You can learn something from everybody and every situation provides an opportunity to become more awake and compassionate. When you embrace your shadow selves and practice acceptance, your compassion can spread to everyone. In this way, you can be grateful to everyone.

Going even deeper, your very existence is dependent upon everybody else. You didn't pop into existence out of nowhere, and you don't live alone in a vacuum. You couldn't be who you are without the entire structure of life around you: your family, relationships and social connections. And you couldn't live without the sustenance the earth provides, the water, food, and air.

Everything that exists is interdependent. Nothing can come into being without everything else. You are who you are because everything is as it is.

For Writers

Have you ever wondered why you write the way you do? Or why you choose to write about a specific subject or character?

Your voice is unique because it reflects who you are. It grows out of the experiences you live through and the relationships that help to form your character. The way you write and the particular stories you want to tell have been imperceptibly influenced by every interaction you have ever had. If you had grown up in a different neighbourhood perhaps you would want to write different stories.

It's not just your personality that is subtly shaped by others. The inspiration for your writing can come from all sorts of unusual places and people too. When you open your life to be grateful to everyone, inspiration can find you from almost anywhere.

And consider where would you be without a shared language and symbolism, the shared understanding of meaning and feeling that allows one person to read another person's writing and be inspired, moved, entertained and transported. You wouldn't be able to read this without access to books, e-readers, computers, pens, paper, an education, and so on. There is really no such thing as an isolated individual. Nothing you do would be possible without the contribution of countless millions of others, mostly unseen and unknown, all around the world.

You may also feel grateful for the opportunity to write and express yourself and create something new. Not everybody is so lucky. If you find yourself in the position where you have a few hours to spare to write a story, remember to be grateful to everyone who has made that possible.

Your gratitude might also extend to the fact that you are alive in the first place, and that you can think and be inspired, and have the opportunity to connect with others.

Exercises

Begin a gratitude journal or diary. Every day write down ten things you're grateful for.

Consider the circumstances and people in your life that support your writing. Write in your journal about the networks of relationships that make your writing possible.

Think about the relationships that helped to form your character growing up, and the relationships you have now in your life. How did these people influence you? Can you identify the effect they have had on your writing?

It's easy to be grateful for positive influences, but now consider the circumstances and people who are not so supportive. Can you find a way to extend gratitude to these influences? What do your difficult relationships reveal about how you feel about yourself? How does this affect your writing?

Slogan 14: Your true Self has the answer

This slogan is about seeing how everything is interconnected and interdependent and using this to wake up to your true Self as Buddha mind. In fact, underneath all the confusion, your ordinary day-to-day mind *is* Buddha mind.

The original slogan is quite technical and needs some explanation: "*Seeing confusion as the four kayas is unsurpassable shunyata protection.*" The four kayas describe the process of awakening. Kayas means 'bodies' and they represent the different ways emptiness (*shunyata*) manifests and how we experience it. (More on Kayas in the glossary)

In simple terms, this means that reality appears to manifest from emptiness but because you take that appearance to be solid and unchanging you end up feeling separate from reality. You hide behind the thick walls of your Ego Fort, which splits your perception into subject and object – you as the subject experiencing the world as object.

This dualistic thinking reinforces the ego and makes you feel like you have to protect yourself from experience, and this creates confusion and suffering. But this slogan is saying that your confusion arises out of emptiness in the same way as everything else. Your perception and experience arise together in the same dance of emptiness as your true Self.

Confusion arises because you keep trying to get hold of reality, to control it and understand it, but it slips through your fingers. Reality never quite makes sense and you end up feeling confused and lost in a maze of thoughts. This slogan says you don't need to get rid of your confusion. Your confusion can become the key to awakening.

If you look into how the mind actually works you can begin to see through the confusion to the reality underneath. When you do that, you see that everything is interdependent. There is no separate self, and following from the last slogan, you know that you depend upon everybody else for your existence.

There is no self and other; it's all Being that manifests in different forms. Everything arises from emptiness, from awareness, and returns there. When you look at your confusion and suffering like this, there is no need to get rid of it because it just evaporates, like mist in the sunshine.

So this slogan encourages you to not take anything personally and not to make an issue out of anything. Whatever happens you can recognise that it all arises from the same place, the same open, spacious emptiness as your true Self or Buddha mind. Don't hold on to your problems or your ideas about reality or awakening. They're all empty, so you can let them go.

> *"There's nothing solid to react to. You have made much ado about nothing."* – Pema Chodron

For Writers

When you spend a lot of time working on a particular project, it's easy to get set in your ways. Perhaps you assume that you know what you're doing and that you know how the story will unfold as you write it. Maybe you think you have created the perfect structure for your novel and that the story can only be told that way, or from one particular perspective.

For example, you might be writing in the first person because you think that's the best way to tell the story. But it's possible you could be wrong. The early drafts of my first novel were written in the third person, bouncing back and forth between the two main characters. It was sloppy and the story felt uneven. It was only later that I realised it would make more sense to tell the story in the first person. After rewriting the entire manuscript from the protagonist's perspective, the story flowed and finally came to life.

Maybe you believe you could never write in a particular medium. For example, if you're a poet, maybe you think prose just uses too many words; or as a novelist you might think limiting yourself to a shorter form would be too challenging. Or perhaps there's a particular subject or genre you would never tackle. Or maybe you believe that you can't write at all and that anything you create is the most horrific waste of paper and time.

None of the above are real problems. The story you're writing doesn't have to happen the way you think it does. Limiting yourself to a shorter form might liberate your creative juices and produce something surprising. Tackling the subject you keep avoiding might give rise to the best work you have ever written. And you don't know if you can write unless you actually give it a go.

Wherever you keep getting stuck, there will be a lot of confusion and doubt, but thinking about it just makes it worse. This slogan encourages you to explore the possibility that you could be wrong, and that you might not have a problem at all. Cut through all the confusion and find alternative possibilities by asking yourself, "*What if I'm wrong?*"

This is especially important if you're stuck in a negative loop of self-doubt and it's stopping you from writing. What if the thought that says you're an idiot who can't write for toffee is wrong?

Listen to your heart for the answer. Your true Self is found in the silence and space of the heart, and if you're right about something, the heart will know. The first voice you hear will probably be the loudest, but that's not the one you want to listen to. The intellect shouts loudly because it's insecure and doesn't really know anything (see Slogan 5). You want to focus on the still small voice of the true Self – that's where your answer will be found.

Exercises

Whenever you feel stuck or confused, not sure what to write or how to fix a problem, turn the problem in on itself and ask: *Who is stuck? Who is confused? Who can't write?* See if you can find the self who thinks it's a writer.

Free write in your journal and watch what happens. While you're writing, see if you can catch yourself in the act. Ask yourself: *Who is writing?*

Slogan 15: Practice the Four Methods

This slogan gives you four practical methods that should form the foundation of your practice. These methods are ways of being in the world that encourage you to face difficult emotions or situations rather than avoid them.

The original slogan is: *"Four practices are the best of methods,"* and these are: (1) do good; (2) avoid evil; (3) welcome mishaps, or mistakes; and (4) pray, or be grateful for the teachings. In simple terms, this means you cultivate compassion and don't cause suffering to yourself or others, while learning from your mistakes and seeking out the best guidance.

Underneath each of these methods is the idea of overcoming resistance. Instead of fighting against difficult circumstances, you turn towards them with compassion and acceptance. Resistance only makes things worse because the more you fight against something, the stronger it gets. So this slogan gives you four methods to overcome that resistance.

In the traditional teachings, **the first method** is called 'accumulating merit,' but it's not just about doing good deeds so you get better karma. Doing good doesn't mean being nice and helping people because it's good for your soul. It may well be good for your soul, but that's not why you do it. You do good because it's an expression of your true nature which is naturally open and compassionate.

So the first method is about doing good without hope of reward or recognition. You get your ego out of the way and do something because it needs to be done, because you want to help. If you're a do-gooder or you give with strings attached, your good deeds won't accumulate merit. This is about the willingness to help others by surrendering your own agenda and being compassionate.

The second method is 'laying down evil deeds.' The word 'evil' might seem like a loaded term, but it just means anything that isn't in your best interests. To avoid evil means to stop doing things that cause you or others to suffer. These are your bad habits and neurotic behaviours, anything driven by fears and doubts caused by not seeing reality clearly.

First you have to notice when you've fallen into a bad habit, and then you need to take steps to make sure it doesn't happen again. You might have to reach a point where you get sick of messing up before things start to change, but it's important that you don't beat yourself up when you get something wrong. Just notice the habit and see if you can find a pattern, a trigger that usually sets you off, and then be willing to cultivate good habits instead. Those good habits will be a natural expression of your true self, which is open and compassionate.

The third method is to welcome mishaps, or 'offering to the döns.' In the traditional teachings, a dön is a malevolent spirit who trips you up and causes problems, but they're doing you a favour because they wake you up. The demons are the negative parts of yourself: bad moods, fear, confusion, selfishness, and so on. So this method is about opening to those moments when things suddenly go wrong – you lose your temper or have an attack of self-doubt or fear. These are opportunities to practice compassion and be kind to yourself.

In the traditional practices, they make an offering of a small cake, or *torma*, to the dön and invite it to come back and visit whenever it likes! This is a way to make friends with your demons and to recognise that they're trying to help you. Mistakes and mishaps keep you on your toes and act as wake-up calls. You're bumping into your own conditioning and the demons are there to make sure you notice.

The final method is to be grateful for the teachings, or 'offering to the dharmapalas.' The dharmapalas are dharma protectors, and you can think of these beings in any way that makes sense to you – God, Buddha, the angels, or your own Higher Self. The protectors act as guardians of awareness and help to keep you connected with something larger than yourself. They are there to remind you that you don't have to struggle with your demons all by yourself. You can ask for help.

However, one of the ways the dharmapalas work is by giving you a nudge when you fall off the path or act in a way that isn't in alignment with your true Self. When you're not mindful, the world will trip you up and something goes wrong. This is instant karma, and it's not always pleasant. I have so many examples of how this works I could fill a whole book with them. For instance, the time I left my flat without paying attention and then discovered I had locked myself out. That woke me up!

Traditionally, the offerings to the protectors involve more cake, but you can practice this method simply by opening yourself to the teachings and being willing to wake up. Just don't be surprised when you get an angelic elbow to the ribs or a finger in the eye when you're caught dozing.

For Writers

When applied to writing practice, the four methods include anything that helps to keep you writing and encourages you to let go of your resistance. The four methods for writers are: (1) write; (2) avoid things that stop you writing; (3) learn from your mistakes; and (4) ask for support.

The first method for writers is obvious. You must write. But forcing yourself to write because you think you should, won't work. You need to write everyday because that's what you want to do. You write because you are a writer. As a writer it is in your nature to write – so write.

The second method for writers is to be aware of anything that gets in the way of your ability to fulfil the first method. Pay attention to the things that stop you from writing, whether they're inside you in the form of doubts and fears, or outside in the form of distractions or difficult circumstances.

Do what you can to minimise the effect of these problems. If you keep getting distracted by the internet, avoid going online – switch off your router or write in a place with no Wi-Fi (although that's getting harder to find these days). If negative thinking or emotions are stopping you from writing, turn those thoughts and feelings into a piece of writing. You may not be able to work on your novel or poem, but you can write about whatever it is that's holding you back. You may even be able to incorporate your demons and darkness into your writing.

The third method for writers is to keep learning from your mistakes. Writing, as they say, is rewriting. You can't write well unless you're willing to evaluate your work and do what is necessary to improve it. When you've spent a long time writing something, it can be disheartening to realise how much more work needs to be done. But mistakes are the only way you learn how to become a better writer, so welcome the opportunity to hone your craft. Sometimes mistakes can even make your work better: an accidental slip up might provide an unexpected image or metaphor that you wouldn't have thought of otherwise. As Dogen reminds us:

"A Zen master's life is one continuous mistake."

The final method for writers is to seek support. Other writers can help to keep you on track by cheering you on and providing support when things aren't going so well. All writers struggle with the same basic problems so knowing that others have the same difficulties helps to keep things in perspective. Other writers can also provide valuable feedback on your writing and help you to improve your work. You can also seek feedback from professional editing services that will help you to make your work the best it can be.

If you follow these four methods you will create an atmosphere around your writing that makes it harder for you to make excuses. This is really about making it as easy as possible for you to write by removing internal and external resistance. That way, the fears of your ego won't have as much ammunition and so they are much less likely to cause you problems.

Exercises

Write something. Right now. No excuses! Put this book down and write for ten minutes. It doesn't matter what you write about, just do it.

In your slogan journal, list all the things that stop you from writing – internal and external. Identify methods you can use to stop those things from stopping you. Create a strategy and put it into practice.

Do some free writing in your journal and try to make as many mistakes as you can. Write the worst thing you have ever written!

Identify a time when a mistake has turned out well. Celebrate your mistakes.

Slogan 16: Whatever you meet is the Path

This slogan is about remembering to be mindful no matter what is happening. Whatever appears in your life, that is what you need to be dealing with because everything you experience can be used to wake you up.

The original slogan is: "*Whatever you meet unexpectedly, join with meditation.*" When things are going well it's easy to practice mindfulness and maintain your focus and peace of mind. Even without paying attention, on a good day you can bimble along and everything goes smoothly, and you can fool yourself that you're on top of things. But when something unexpected happens it becomes more of a challenge to stay focused and maintain your poise.

Unexpected disruptions to your routine can be positive or negative, but either way, they can throw you off your game. When something good happens out of the blue you get caught up in the excitement and you're off in a whirlwind of celebration and happiness. There's nothing wrong with this – of course you should enjoy your successes – but you can get so distracted that you stop paying attention, and that's when you end up accidentally tripping yourself up.

Or your life is running smoothly and everything is great, and then an unexpected problem comes up that forces you to stop in your tracks. You get angry at the disruption and take it as a personal insult. Things were going so well, how could this terrible thing be happening, and now, of all times? Interruptions and distractions never happen at a convenient moment.

The truth is that life is always changing in unpredictable ways. If you think that practising mindfulness will turn your life into one long peaceful glide through perfect experiences, you're going to be disappointed. At some point, the path ahead will become rocky or take a few detours in unexpected directions, and it won't be long before you're falling over yourself trying to keep up.

You may like to believe that if you could just control your mind and keep it nice and calm, that your life will go the same way. But you can't control reality with your beliefs. When life throws you a curve ball, there's no point in getting angry at it. If you were really paying attention, you would simply catch the ball and carry on.

So this slogan reminds you not to get carried away by your assumptions about what's going on and to not let your habits take over. Even positive habits, like practising mindfulness, can become routine and automatic. Then along comes an unexpected disruption to wake you up. You can welcome these interruptions and distractions as opportunities to practice being present. Don't let your routines become a kind of autopilot, and remember: there's no excuse for not practising mindfulness.

For Writers

There are three levels to this slogan for writers. The first is obvious: how to deal with the times you get distracted by interruptions to your writing routine. You're sitting at your desk, writing happily, when the phone rings, or there's an unexpected problem that needs fixing in your life and it pulls you away from writing. This is covered by another slogan: *Practice when you're distracted*, so we'll deal with that then.

The next level addresses unexpected changes in your writing career. Perhaps you've been writing for a long time but haven't managed to break through into getting your work published, and then suddenly you find yourself with a book deal. Now there are other people with a stake in your work and the expectations of readers to fulfil. These are wonderful problems to have, but the danger is that your relationship to your own writing will change as a result. Can you maintain a deep connection to your own voice while under pressure to perform by the publisher and still produce books that sell?

Or perhaps you've had years of success and your books have done well, but they're no longer selling the way they used to. Suddenly, your publisher decides it doesn't want to publish your next book and you're out on your own again. How do you come to terms with your publisher's loss of confidence in your ability to sell? Do you let it interfere with your ability to write the stories that you want to tell?

Whatever the ups and downs of your writing career, this slogan reminds you to meet it with mindfulness, to apply the clarity of your open mind and compassion to the situation in which you find yourself. There's no easy response to these unexpected detours, but stepping back and taking the time to meditate on what you're feeling will help you to find an appropriate way forward – and to keep writing.

The deepest level of this slogan builds on the last, and reminds you that anything that happens in your life can be used to deepen your understanding of yourself and your writing. Whether the experiences are good or bad, it doesn't matter. It's all grist for the mill.

Even if you get so distracted by problems that it stops you from writing, deep down, you're still on the path. Your stuckness, confusion, and fears are all part of what it means to be you, so they can all go into your writing. Instead of getting angry with things that stop you from writing, turn towards them and explore what they might be trying to tell you. If you're too confused or scared to write – write about your fear and why you're confused.

This slogan is saying that no matter what you're going through, or have been through, you can use it in your writing. There's no need to hold anything back. Everything that happens to you shapes the way you write and the kinds of stories you choose to tell. Even if you avoid certain experiences or try to hide what you're really feeling, it will be revealed in your choices as you write.

This slogan encourages you to stay with yourself no matter what happens, and to keep writing whatever unexpected twists and detours appear on the path ahead.

Exercises

In your slogan journal, plot out your writing career to date with all its ups and downs. Is there a pattern to the way you work? Do you allow yourself to get distracted by unexpected detours?

Look at every story, poem, or piece of work you have written. Did you finish it? If not, why not?

Identify the experiences you've had that influenced your desire to be a writer. Why do you write the way you do?

Slogan 17: Practice the Five Strengths

This slogan is about making a commitment to build positive habits that reinforce your connection with your true Self. When you do this it will help you to overcome the fears and doubts of your ego, and to live in a more openhearted and compassionate way.

The original slogan is: *"Practice the five strengths, the condensed heart instructions."* The heart instructions are the Buddha's teachings, and the five strengths are a distillation of the most important points. These are:

- Determination
- Familiarisation
- Positive Seed or Virtue
- Reproach
- Aspiration

The five strengths are about taking your mind training practice seriously and empowering yourself to remember who you really are. They help to keep you motivated and focused on what matters to you.

Determination means making a commitment to your highest goals and consciously choosing what you're going to do. It's about making an effort to actually do what you say you want to do and not to just drift through life and get sidetracked by things that don't matter. Whatever you want to do will take determination to keep going for as long as it takes to get it done.

Familiarisation is about creating positive habits that reinforce your determination to achieve your goals. This means that your mind training and mindfulness practice becomes a familiar part of your life. They're not just something extra you add onto a list of things to do, but part of the way you live your life. Mind training and meditation need to become as much a part of your daily routine as cleaning your teeth or eating breakfast. You take the teachings into yourself so they become an intimate part of your life.

Positive Seed is about remembering who you really are. It's also called the Seed of Virtue and the idea is to nurture this seed that exists in you. This is your Buddha nature or true Self. As you practice mind training, this part of your self will become stronger and clearer. It's already there, buried deep inside you – all you have to do is let it grow by encouraging it to sprout with your determination and familiarisation.

Reproach is about recognising that you can be your own worst enemy. You can see how your ego and its stories get you into trouble, so you reproach the ego. In other words, you turn away from being driven by fear and doubt. But it's important that you don't start beating yourself up when you notice a bad habit is causing problems. Just stop taking your faults and failures so personally. Notice them and recognise where you've gone wrong, but do it with kindness and humour. "*Oops, there I go again!*" and turn back to the positive seed with determination.

Aspiration is about reaffirming your desire to awaken and live in a more compassionate way. If you think about where you're likely to end up if you keep going without changing the way you live, that can give you a powerful motivation to aspire to do better. Make a vow to remember that you're practising not just for yourself, but for the benefit of others too.

This slogan encourages you to be intentional about what you're doing, to really think about what you're trying to achieve, and to make an effort to stick to your intentions. But this doesn't mean you have to force things or work really hard to make things go the way you want. It's more about trusting your true Self, your positive seed, and opening to the possibility of awakening. You don't have to struggle and fight, you just have to be willing to try your best.

For Writers

This slogan gives you a challenge: either you want to write, or you don't. Writing isn't a chore. It's not an added extra that you have to fit into your day. If writing is important to you, then you need to take it seriously. Practising the five strengths can help:

Determination means making a commitment to your writing. Don't keep putting it off or allow yourself to get sidetracked by distractions and unnecessary activities, like cleaning the oven for the umpteenth time. Stop procrastinating and get on with it. The only way your writing will get done is if you actually sit down and write. You could motivate yourself by writing your own personal manifesto stating your writing goals and intentions.

Familiarisation means creating good habits that help you to incorporate writing into your daily life. Take a realistic look at your routines and work out how you can make the time to commit to a daily writing practice. It might mean giving up some activities – things that aren't as important to you as writing, such as social media – or rescheduling them. Regardless of whatever else you have to do, if you want to write, then you have to write every day.

Positive Seed means remembering who you are. In this case, it means remembering you're a writer. And what do writers do? They write. Nurture your desire to write by cultivating practices and positive daily habits that support your writing.

Reproach means recognising when your ego gets in the way of your writing. But instead of giving yourself a hard time when you don't write, just notice what has happened and call it out: *"It's that pesky procrastination again!"* or *"Hello self-doubt, back again I see!"* Then let it go and remember your positive seed, your desire to write. Turn away from anything that stops you from writing. This doesn't mean other people, unless they're actively stopping you from writing; it means you turn away from ego trips and avoidance and internal emotional blockages that are holding you back.

Aspiration means reaffirming your desire to write, but it can also mean having the aspiration to become a better writer. You may want to aspire to getting published or being a successful writer, but those are things you can't control because they involve other people. You can only control how hard you're willing to work on your writing. So aim high – but aim to write as well as you can. Your readers will thank you for it.

Exercises

Identify your writing goals and intentions and write your own writing manifesto. You can write it in your journal or print it out so you can hang it above your desk where you can see it every day.

Create a realistic writing schedule for the next week and make sure you stick to it.

In your slogan journal, identify the things that get in the way of your writing. List your top five emotional complexes – you might even like to give them names. Practice calling them out when you spot them in action.

Feed your aspiration by taking a class or reading up on a point of craft that will help improve your writing.

Slogan 18: Don't waste your life

This slogan is about facing up to your mortality and remembering not to take your life for granted. The original slogan is rather long and relates to the previous slogan too: *"The mahayana instruction for ejection of consciousness at death is the five strengths: how you conduct yourself is important."*

The five strengths introduced in Slogan 17 are instructions on how to live, and this slogan is about practising for death, but the two are interconnected. How you feel about death influences how you live, and how you live will influence how you eventually die. To die well means to have lived well. To live well comes back to the five strengths and the importance of not drifting through life or wasting the precious opportunity you have to wake up and be really present.

We don't like the idea of death. You may pretend to yourself that you'll live forever, that somehow this terrible fate will pass you by. But deep down, you know that's not possible. In fact, the idea of living forever is worse than dying, although not everyone would agree. Death puts your life into perspective and encourages you to make the most of whatever time you have. But you can't do that if you're scared of dying.

Even if you're not consciously worried about death, it's there in the background, and not just the idea of your own death or the people you love. Everything ends sooner or later, and nothing lasts forever. The fact that everything changes can be difficult to accept, and this fear can influence your behaviour whether you realise it or not.

One of your ego's main fears is that you're not safe, so you spend a lot of time and energy defending yourself and trying to make yourself feel better. This can be subtle or obvious, but it happens because you feel separate from life. Whenever anything happens that you can't control – which is most of the time – you feel threatened and this can make you close down or withdraw from living your life to the full.

This slogan reminds you not to waste your life. The five strengths give you a way to face life and death with equanimity and stay open to change rather than shutting down. Using determination, familiarisation, positive seed, reproach, and aspiration, you can live in an intentional way rather than drifting towards death. The point of the five strengths is to use every moment you have to wake up, and you can't do that if you're scared to live because you're scared of dying.

Since you're going to die either way, why can't you just drift through life and take it easy? Why is waking up so important?

Living intentionally and doing all you can to wake up is important because the alternative means your life is controlled by fear. That's not an easy way to live. When you wake up, you can choose how to live, no matter what happens in your life. You can choose to change your attitude and free yourself from the fears that hold you back and stop you from enjoying life.

For Writers

Life can end at any moment. The odds are that you will live a long time, but you really don't know. This slogan is a reminder that you don't know how much time you have left to live.

Every moment is precious, every day is a fresh opportunity to try again or do something new. You don't want to reach the end of your life and find yourself full of regret for all the things you didn't do because you were too scared to take a risk. Life is full of risk. If you try to live in a way that avoids anything that might kill you – it would probably kill you!

But fear of death isn't the only thing that can stop you living a full life. There are multiple fears that can haunt a writer: fear of failure, fear of success, fear of humiliation, fear of being ignored, fear of being talentless, fear that all your fears will come true – the list is endless.

Underneath all these fears is the fear of loss of control, that you won't be able to handle whatever happens, that one way or another, it will be the end of you – i.e. death.

If you allow these fears to control the way you live, you'll never get any writing done. Or the writing you do will always fall short of what you imagine it could be, if only you could stop feeling so scared. This slogan reminds you that your time is limited and your life is precious.

Don't be one of those writers who say they want to write a novel, but never actually does. Whenever you notice yourself pulling back from an opportunity or doubting your ability to write or achieve your goals, this slogan can bring you back to the present moment. Don't waste your life worrying about things you can't control.

Not writing won't kill you, but it will make you miserable. There's nothing worse than wanting to write but being too scared to try. There's only one way to find out if you can do something, and that's to give it a go. Just write and see what happens. What's the worst that could happen?

Life and death are mysteries. Nobody really understands what's going on or what life ultimately means. But if you close yourself off to the mystery because you're scared of death, or scared to live fully because it's painful, then your writing will be cramped and limited accordingly.

Opening to the mystery will reduce the power of your fears and open up your writing. You'll be more willing to take risks and try things you might usually avoid. Face your mortality now and your life will be full of appreciation for the mystery, and you'll be less likely to waste your time on things that don't ultimately matter.

Exercises

In your slogan journal, make a list of all the fears you have about your writing.

From your list, identify the most powerful fear and imagine the worst has happened. Spend some time free writing on this fear and how you would deal with it.

What are you scared to write? In your journal, write about the subjects that frighten you or the styles of writing you're scared to try. Why do they scare you?

Take a risk. Do something today that you would never normally do.

Slogan 19: Get over yourself

This slogan captures the essence of mind training, which is to realise who you really are and get your ego out of the way. It helps you to remember that the world doesn't revolve around you.

The original slogan is: "*All dharma agrees at one point.*" In other words, all spiritual practices and teachings are ultimately about the same thing – to let go of your ego. Sometimes this is called 'ego death', but that's not strictly accurate. It can't be killed because it doesn't inherently exist, and as we'll see, what the ego is made from is pure illusion, so the idea of killing the ego doesn't make much sense.

The ego is the main obstacle on the spiritual path, but that doesn't mean it's a bad thing. It's important to develop a healthy ego and sense of self as you grow up because you need to be able to relate to the world as an individual. The problems start when you hold on to your ego too tightly.

The ego is made from stories. It's all the stories you tell yourself about who you think you are, or 'should' be or would like to be. The ego isn't necessarily a 'bad guy', but it does have a tendency to hijack whatever you're doing and try to take control – and take the credit when things happen to go the way you want. It does this because it is fundamentally insecure.

The ego is insecure because it's a defensive structure. You want to feel safe and secure in a changing and unpredictable world, so you build an Ego Fort and pull up the drawbridge to hide behind the walls of your fear and doubt. But this can make you rigid and controlling, even if it's only subtle. You don't have to be a total control freak to have problems when life doesn't go your way.

The more attached you are to your ego and the stories it tells, the harder it is to deal with reality when things 'go wrong.' You want life to be a certain way, but life won't cooperate, so the ego is always going to be insecure.

There's only one way around this problem and that's to get over yourself. Stop clinging to your desire to have life go the way you want and open yourself up to the possibility that reality isn't about you.

For Writers

This slogan encourages you to get out of your own way and let the writing write itself. When you cling too fiercely to the stories you tell about yourself, it blocks your ability to hear the quieter voice of your true Self, but that is where your writing voice comes from.

The ego's voice is usually the loudest. Driven by fear and insecurity, it shouts to get your attention and to make sure you do what's necessary to make it feel safe. But if every time you sit down to write all you can hear are the voices of doubt going round and round inside your head, you'll be lucky to write anything at all.

This slogan can help you to ignore the voice of fear when it tries to distract you. When doubt takes over, turn it around and reflect it back on itself. Doubt your doubts. If your ego thinks you can't write (because it's secretly scared of failure, for example), question that thought and pull it apart. You can't know whether you can write, or not, if you don't actually try to write. So get over yourself and write anyway.

This slogan can also mean you should avoid being self-absorbed in your writing. If you're tempted to include too much of your own experience in a story, for example, remembering to get over yourself will help to get 'you' out of the way. Then you can let the story breathe, and let the characters speak for themselves.

Too much ego can also mean that you try to control your writing too much, due to anxiety and doubts – like worrying what others will think of it or whether your writing will sell. This can make it hard to write fluently because you're constantly second guessing what you want to say. Get over yourself so you can clear your mind of fears and write without your ego hijacking the whole process.

Exercises

What does your Ego Fort look like? Draw a picture in your slogan journal.

In your slogan journal, list all the ways you doubt your writing. Now work down the list and doubt each of your doubts – turn them inside out and deconstruct them.

To practice getting over yourself, do some free writing in your journal about what you're worried others will think of you and/or your writing. When you're finished, go through the same process of deconstruction, and remember: they're just stories – you don't have to believe them.

Slogan 20: Trust yourself

This slogan is about remembering that only you know what's right for you. Only you know if you are doing your best because only you have a direct line to your deepest truth.

The original slogan is: *"Of the two witnesses, hold the principal one."* The two witnesses are you and other people, but you are the principal one. So this slogan is telling you to rely on your own perspective. It's not that you shouldn't seek advice or guidance from others, just that in the end, you have to decide what's right for you.

Sometimes it's hard to trust yourself because you can't see yourself clearly. A lot of your behaviour is unconscious and driven by hidden fears and doubts, so others can often see things in you that you can't see yourself, such as positive or negative characteristics and potentials. Because of this, it's worth listening to what others have to say – you might learn something useful about yourself.

On the other hand, we rarely see each other as we really are because our perception is coloured by assumptions and unconscious projections. When you meet somebody for the first time you make judgements and assumptions about the kind of person you think they are. Some of that will be accurate and some of it won't. You put them in a box in your mind and it can be very hard to change your opinion of them once it's formed.

So when others see you, they're looking at you through the imaginary box inside their head. And you're doing the same to them. It's a wonder we manage to communicate at all.

The way we relate to each other is full of these grey areas of confusion and mixed messages. No matter how close you may be with somebody, there is always an unbridgeable gap between your experience of yourself and their experience of you. But you have a better chance of coming to understand and see yourself more clearly than they do. Because no matter how well somebody knows you, they will never know you as well as you can know yourself.

This throws you back on yourself and your own judgement. You can take advice and listen to what others have to say, but ultimately, you have to work out who you are and how to live your life. Whatever you decide, you're the one who will have to live with the consequences. You are alone.

If you want to avoid that responsibility, then your life will be dictated by the values and desires of others. But living that way is guaranteed to make you miserable. Worrying what others think of you makes you doubt yourself and drives you to seek their approval. But the more you do that, the harder it is to trust yourself.

In the end, you have no choice but to be true to yourself because you are the only authority on your own life. Ask yourself what the approval of somebody else means if they don't know you? Real trust and understanding can only come from the depths of your own soul.

When it comes to choosing how to live, what you value, and what you need in order to feel happy and alive, there is only one expert you can rely on – you. Nobody has ever been you before in the history of existence, so nobody can tell you that you're doing it wrong. Nobody can say that you're being you the wrong way. How would they know?

You are the expert on you. Trust yourself.

For Writers

This slogan is a reminder that only you know what you should be writing at any given time. When you turn inwards, there are stories and ideas bubbling away in your subconscious and you have to decide which ones you're going to give your attention to. How you make those choices depends on your reasons for writing in the first place:

Are you writing to see your work in print, or just to please yourself? Do you want to sell your writing in the marketplace, or are you more interested in exploring your own ideas? Or perhaps you want to write something that expresses your true voice and reaches a wider audience.

These aren't easy questions to answer, but only you know what you need to write and which stories need to be told. They're the ones you can't stop thinking about, the ones that wake you up in the middle of the night, buzzing with ideas and possibilities. If you trust yourself, you'll write the right stories. Others may not agree with you, but you're the one who has to do the work.

You also have to trust yourself when it comes to the quality of your writing. Deep down you know when you're not writing well enough – you can feel it. If you find yourself wincing or cringing when you read back something you've written, it's a sure sign it needs more work. Learn to trust your inner compass and follow your own judgement on whether your writing is good enough.

You can't ignore the opinions of others completely – you will need to seek advice and feedback on your writing, but you must also decide which of others' views are worth taking into consideration. Not all feedback is genuinely useful and some of it can be downright destructive. Although it's often the case that others can perceive your writing voice more easily than you can.

It can be tricky to get the balance right and not become too self-critical. But in the end, only you know if you are writing to the best of your ability. Only you know what your writing intentions and goals are and whether you are working consistently towards them.

Exercises

Revisit your writing manifesto from Slogan 17. If you didn't write one then, do it now! Are you living up to your intentions and goals?

In your slogan journal, write about how you can tell when you're writing well. What does it feel like?

If you struggle to trust yourself, can you identify why that might be? Meditate on your lack of self-belief and write any insights in your slogan journal.

Practice tonglen with the fears and doubts that prevent you from trusting yourself. Do this every day until you feel able to believe in yourself again.

Slogan 21: Always maintain a joyful mind

This slogan is a reminder not to take yourself too seriously. The original slogan is more or less the same: *"Always maintain only a joyful mind,"* which means that no matter what is going on, you can have an optimistic approach to life.

On the surface, it seems callous to suggest that you should always be joyful. There is so much trouble and suffering in the world; how can you be happy when there are others in pain?

It seems simplistic too – as if you could solve all your problems by cheering up. This slogan is especially hard to understand if you're not particularly happy right now or struggling with painful experiences. There's nothing worse than being told to cheer up when you're feeling depressed.

But this slogan isn't about pretending to be happy when you're not, or forcing yourself to think or feel a certain way. It's just a gentle prod to remind you not to lose your perspective. Don't take yourself or the process of training your mind too seriously.

Often when you try to achieve something, there's a tendency to push too hard for success. You want it so much, that you try too hard. The insecurity of the ego makes you doubt yourself, so you go to the opposite extreme and take it all too seriously. You hold on too tight and fight for what you want.

But this slogan is saying: *take it easy – you'll get there!*

You don't have to hold on or fight to get what you want. The fact that you even have the opportunity to practice mind training and meditation at all is a great gift. You can afford to lighten up. This doesn't mean you don't care about the suffering of others or the problems of the world, or even your own suffering. It just means that you can loosen your grip and smile. You can keep your sense of humour, even when things aren't going well.

Because underneath it all, the truth is that Buddha mind is a joyful mind. And you are Buddha mind – that is your true nature.

So relax – you're closer to home than you realise.

For Writers

This slogan reminds you not to beat yourself up when your writing isn't going well. When you get stuck and don't know what to write, or when your novel is rejected (again!), it's hard to feel positive about your writing. There may be days when you wonder why you bother to write at all.

Writing can be hard work and sometimes you get precious little support or encouragement. It's easy to get bogged down in negativity. But this slogan gives you a friendly nudge and says: *lighten up!*

You don't have to write. Nobody is forcing you to do it! So if you're not enjoying it, stop.

On the other hand, perhaps you're not enjoying it because you're taking either yourself or the writing too seriously. Rejection will happen, no matter how well you write. You'll have bad days when the words don't flow and everything you write makes you doubt your grasp of the language. But that's okay.

Writing is a process. Tomorrow you can try again. This slogan reminds you of the most important thing – that writing is meant to be fun. It's play. So when you're not enjoying it, take a break and get back in touch with your enthusiasm and your joy, and have some fun.

Taking a break away from your desk is a good idea for other reasons too. Your posture affects your mood, and if you spend a lot of time hunched over a desk you can become tense without even realising. A lack of exercise can also affect your mood. It's easy to fall into a negative frame of mind, even without professional disappointments or adverse circumstances.

So doing something as simple as sitting up straight and going for a walk every day, could help you to maintain a joyful mind – and that will have a direct impact on the quality of your writing. At the very least, you'll enjoy it more.

Exercises

In your slogan journal, write about why you enjoy writing. What are your favourite types of stories, and why?

While you're writing, check for tension in your body:
- Where are your shoulders – are they hunched up by your ears?
- Are you frowning as you concentrate?
- What about your neck, back, legs, and belly?

Make a point of relaxing your shoulders and facial muscles when you sit down to write and check in with yourself regularly.

Go for a walk! Seriously – stop reading this and get some exercise.

Have some fun!

Slogan 22: Practice when you're distracted

This slogan is about remembering the discipline of mindfulness and not allowing yourself to get distracted. The original slogan is: "*If you can practice even when distracted, you are well trained.*" So even your distractions can become part of your mind training practice.

The mind is highly distractible. This is why meditation and mindfulness are so difficult, because the mind naturally moves – incessantly. It never stops. So when you sit down to meditate, the mind often reacts to the stillness and silence by going absolutely ballistic.

The way the mind constantly leaps about is normal – there's nothing wrong with you for thinking this way. In the past it would have helped us to stay alert to possible threats while out hunting sabre-toothed tigers and mammoths, it kept us on our evolutionary toes. Without the distractibility of the mind we wouldn't have survived for long.

This slogan acknowledges the fact that you can't stop the mind from being distracted; it's going to happen. It's in the nature of the mind to be distracted, so you have to work with it. This will take discipline and patience; you can't expect instant results. So you have no choice but to practice when you're distracted, i.e. all the time.

As distractible as the mind is, it's also very good at focusing on one thing at a time – if you train it.

In fact, you wouldn't get distracted in the first place if you weren't aware. Every distraction can become a reminder, a pointer towards the truth of who you are. Awareness is your natural state, so distractions can be used to bring your attention back to the awareness in which the distraction arises.

When you're meditating, notice when your mind wanders and bring it back. As you go about your day, notice when you're getting scattered and distracted by the multiple demands on your time and attention, and take a moment to focus on who is being distracted. Ask yourself, "*Who is aware?*"

For Writers

Distractions are one of the biggest causes of procrastination for writers, but you don't have to give in to them. If you really want to write, you will find a way to deal with the daily distractions in your life. You don't have to write with your phone on your desk or with the internet on in the background. You can choose to switch them off and focus on your work.

The real question then, is why you allow yourself to be distracted in this way. Are you using the many distractions of modern life as an excuse? If so, for what?

You will never find or create the perfect circumstances in which to write. Life is messy and changeable, and you can never predict what will happen next. You will never be able to completely empty your mind or your life of distractions and problems. You will have to write in spite of these things.

This slogan encourages you to write through the distractions. Don't use them as excuses to avoid writing, and don't wait for life to provide perfect distraction-free time for you to play with your muse. You can't wait for the muse, or silence – you have to write anyway.

Practice staying focused and committed to your work even when your life is full of distractions. Mindfully deal with your daily routines, the comings and goings, and the technology that eats into your attention and time. Switch off your phone and the internet, if it helps.

And if you tend to use distractions as an excuse to avoid writing – write anyway. Write when you don't feel like writing. Write when you have problems in your life. Write when you doubt yourself. Write even when you think you can't write – write about why you think you can't write, at least then you're writing something.

Whatever happens – write anyway.

Exercises

In your slogan journal, write about the major causes of distraction in your life. Include outer and inner distractions.

Are you using distractions as an excuse to avoid writing? Be honest. Meditate on what you're running away from, and then write your insights in your journal.

If you're used to peace and quiet, practice writing amidst chaos. Put the TV on in the background, go to a noisy café or deliberately sit somewhere you know you'll be interrupted or disrupted. Ask someone to annoy you at regular intervals!

Slogan 23: Come back to basics

This slogan is about making and keeping a commitment to your mind training practice. Up until now the slogans have focused on working with your mind, but from this slogan onwards they're about putting that training into practice with others.

The original slogan is: *"Always abide by the three basic principles,"* which are to keep your promises, to not act outrageously, and to develop patience. All three basic principles are about self-mastery and overcoming the tendency to get sidetracked by your ego.

The first principle is to keep your promises and honour your commitments. Mind training can be hard work and it's easy to flake out or give up when it gets difficult. So you need to stick to your commitment and keep practising.

In the traditional teachings, the first principle is about keeping the promises you make in the refuge and bodhisattva vows. **The refuge vow** means committing to your own awakening. You do this by taking refuge in the Buddha, the Dharma, and the sangha.

By taking refuge in the Buddha you recognise that you have Buddha nature and that this is your guide to how you should live. The Dharma is the Buddha's teachings, and the sangha is the community of fellow practitioners. Making a commitment to mind training and awakening within a community helps you to keep your vows because your spiritual friends will keep you accountable.

The bodhisattva vow is about making a commitment to awaken for the sake of others. You work on your own mind so you can help others to do the same. This is about sharing your wisdom and compassion and recognising that you're not just doing this for yourself because everybody is interconnected.

The second principle is to not act outrageously. If you're following the bodhisattva path then your desire to help others can become distorted by the ego if you're not careful. You're no better than others just because you're on the spiritual path. If you want to help others, then your focus should be on them, not your spiritual progress.

This is about not seeking attention for what you're doing and not showing off or boasting about your accomplishments. Don't brag about how long you can sit in meditation, for example, or make an issue about how good or spiritual you are. The need to be seen as special or talented or wise or spiritual is an ego trip. This process isn't about you; remember Slogan 19.

The third principle is to develop patience. Mind training takes a long time and you'll probably never achieve complete command over your own mind. To do that would mean being a Zen master or something similar, a full-blown Buddha, and that isn't easy. Well, it is easy if you're a master, but getting there is hard. So accept this process will take a while and be patient.

There's no rush. It's not a race and you don't have to prove yourself.

For Writers

This slogan is about making and keeping a commitment to your writing practice. So the three basic principles for writers are to keep your promises, to be modest, and to be patient.

Remember the commitment you made to your writing at the beginning of this process with the first slogan. You promised yourself that you would write. This slogan reminds you of that promise and of your intention to train your mind to free yourself from the fears that stop you from writing the way you want to.

Writing well is hard work and there will be times when it feels as if it's not worth the effort. Use this slogan to remind you of your commitment on those days when you feel like giving up. Yes, it's hard work but you will only improve with practice. You made a promise to yourself – stick to it and keep writing.

The second principle reminds you to be modest about your work. Writing isn't about showing off or trying to impress people with your perfectly crafted prose and evocative use of metaphor. Don't think that you're better than others because you're a writer and they're not, or because your books sell more than theirs, or you have more fans or followers on social media, and so on.

Writing well isn't really about you. It's about making it easier for others to connect with your work and understand what you're saying. Writing is about communication, and you can't communicate effectively if you think you're better than others. Nobody enjoys being patronised. Never underestimate your readers and never talk down to them.

To write well you must have patience. It takes a long time to become a good writer, to understand your own voice and know how to let your strengths shine while working on your limitations. The development of a writing career usually takes decades. Some writers get lucky with their first novel, but for most it takes many years of hard work and rejection before their writing is accepted as good enough.

The process of writing a novel, story or poem also takes time. The process of discovering an idea and exploring character and trying out possibilities requires a willingness to allow a story to breathe and develop in its own way. You can't rush this and sometimes you have to wait for an idea to mature before you can give it the right form.

Finally, if you want to sell your work, then at some point you will have to deal with the business side of writing. This is where the need for patience really takes centre stage. It can take years to find the right agent, editor, or publisher for your work, and even once you have achieved that, you'll still be waiting for the slow wheels of the publishing machine to turn and for your book to appear in the shops.

Exercises

Revisit your intentions from Slogan 1 and answer these questions in your slogan journal: Why did you commit to writing? Why is it so important to you?

Make a promise to yourself to keep writing. Write it down in a one-sentence statement and pin it up near your writing desk. For example, this by Clarissa Pinkola Estés:

> *"I love my creative life more than I love cooperating with my own oppression."*

Slogan 24: Don't be a fake

This slogan is a reminder not to become egotistical about trying to transcend your ego. Mind training aims to free you from the tyranny of the ego and its fears, but there is no need to turn that process into another ego trip.

The original slogan is: *"Change your attitude, but remain natural."* The change in attitude refers to letting go of your ego, and remaining natural means staying true to who you really are. So as you free yourself from the negative habits in your mind, don't turn your new perspective into another kind of ego identity.

When you are centred on your ego it means you're focused on yourself and how you feel, rather than on having compassion for others. This can be blatant self-promotion, such as believing you're better than others, or it can be neurotic and driven by low self-esteem.

When you're neurotic, you don't believe you're better than others, but because you don't like yourself, you tend to seek others' approval or try to make them like you by being extra nice or good. But this is just as self-centred and egotistical as somebody who is always putting themselves first.

The problem in both these cases is the same: too much focus on the ego. The confident egotist wants to maintain their perceived supremacy, and their feeling of being in control and the centre of attention. While the insecure egotist just wants to feel better about themselves. But both of these approaches are fake.

To remain natural means to be true to your deeper Self, your true nature. This is who you are naturally, before you get twisted out of shape by your ego's stories and shenanigans. In terms of spiritual practice, this means there's no need to try hard to 'be spiritual.'

If you let go of your ego but then impose a new set of rules on yourself about how you should behave now that you're officially 'a spiritual person,' all you're doing is creating a new ego identity, a new story to live inside. It might be a more enjoyable, happier story, one with less fears and hang-ups, but in the end, you're still trying too hard.

You don't have to try in order to be you. You can relax and the truth of who you are is there.

For Writers

This slogan is a reminder to write from your soul, not from your ego.

When you first start to write, you often begin by imitating others or copying their style. Until you feel comfortable with your own voice, that can be a good way to learn the craft and practice writing. But at some point you will have to come out of hiding and write something that only you can write.

How do you find your voice as a writer? By relaxing. Your voice will come through as soon as you stop worrying what others will think of your work. You don't have to write the way others say you should write. You need to write the way only you can, by drawing on your unique set of characteristics and experiences.

This doesn't necessarily mean you must only 'write what you know.' You write what only you could imagine. Your prose style and the stories and characters that you're interested in exploring, all come from the depths of your own being. Most of your influences will be unconscious. But if you're frightened of what might be lurking in the depths, you will have trouble relaxing enough to trust yourself to write fluently. Hence the need for mind training.

This slogan reminds you not to hide behind your ego's defences or avoid saying what you need to say or writing the way you need to write. An authentic voice always carries more weight than a fake one. If you want to connect with your readers, give them something real. Give them you.

This slogan can also mean you don't have to approach your writing the way others say you should. For example, if somebody says you must write 1,000 words a day, you don't necessarily have to impose that upon yourself.

However you write, it should fit your lifestyle and schedule. It's not always possible to write as much as you would like, but beating yourself up because you're not living up to somebody else's standards isn't going to help. Find your own ways of working that are true to you, and don't allow yourself to be dictated to by others or by your own anxiety, self-doubt or guilt.

Finally, this slogan can also be about not selling out. If you are lucky enough to have the opportunity to publish your writing on a commercial basis, you may be tempted to change your work for the sake of the marketplace. There is nothing wrong with making your work as good as it can be, and that can involve a lot of compromises, but you may also be encouraged to make changes that don't feel authentic.

Under those circumstances, you would have to decide how far you are willing to go in order to be published. Is it worth losing your authentic voice? How would you feel if you were to end up locked into a contract to write multiple books that don't reflect your true values and voice? Only you can answer these questions, but this slogan encourages you to remain true to yourself.

Exercises

In your slogan journal, write about the kinds of stories you want to tell. Look through the writing you have done, including any unfinished works, and see if you can find a pattern. Are there particular subjects you keep returning to? Or certain types of character or plot?

The best way to discover your voice is through free writing. Pick a favourite subject and write in your journal for 20 – 30 minutes. Don't censor yourself or worry about making sense – just write. Do this regularly, every day if you can, and your true voice will begin to shine through the noise.

What is your USP? A Unique Selling Point is something that you have and others don't. What is unique about your writing? Explore the possibilities in your journal.

Slogan 25: Don't criticise

This slogan is about not criticising others in order to feel better about yourself. The original slogan is: *"Don't talk about injured limbs,"* which challenges you to accept people as they are, warts and all.

Criticising others is one of the ways the ego tries to make itself feel better. It's part of your conditioning and easy to slip into automatically. The ego wants to protect itself from threats and fears, and uses criticism as a smokescreen. You may not even realise you're trying to build yourself up by putting others down. Your criticism may be obvious, as in a verbal attack or laughing at somebody, for example. But it can also be as subtle as the embarrassment caused by not knowing how to deal with difference, looking away a little too fast, or making a polite excuse to leave – the whole fraught landscape of political correctness.

This slogan asks you to notice those moments when you subtly, or not so subtly, judge others and reject them, and to recognise it as an opportunity to practice compassion. It also applies to those moments when you become irritated by somebody else's behaviour, perhaps because they have let you down or hurt you in some way.

This doesn't mean you should put up with bad behaviour or avoid challenging somebody who is being abusive or difficult. But if you want to help a person to change their behaviour, criticism will have the opposite effect because it only draws attention to the problem. Criticism throws a spotlight on a person's weakness or failure, and magnifies it. Shaming somebody into changing never works.

When somebody behaves badly it's usually because they are suffering, and criticism will just make the situation worse. Focusing on what is wrong with someone, or different about them, reduces them to that one characteristic – they become nothing but their bad temper, for example. But people are more than their weaknesses.

There's a story behind every moment, every slip of the tongue, every mistake, every failure. Your weakness, ugliness, clumsiness, and frailty are all part of your humanity. Nobody is perfect and everybody is doing the best they can under the circumstances. When you criticise somebody, you don't know what they're going through. Criticising them for failing to live up to an ideal in your head about how others should look or behave is nonsensical. Turn it around and imagine how you would feel if somebody did that to you, and remember that you're not perfect either.

This slogan encourages you to accept others as they are, just as you would like people to accept you as you are.

It can also be a reminder to not criticise yourself. When you make a mistake or fail or just have a bad day, don't be too hard on yourself. You don't have to be perfect – you just have to be you.

For Writers

This slogan is tricky to navigate for writers. You can't avoid criticising your own writing. You have to look at your work and judge if it could be improved, but you can do that in a way that isn't harsh or destructive.

This slogan doesn't mean you should avoid critiquing your work or tell yourself that every word you write is pure gold. Use it as a reminder to be constructive. When you're editing and rewriting your work, keep your criticism focused on the writing and don't turn it against yourself. Don't become your own worst critic. Remember that you will only improve if you make mistakes and that every mistake is an opportunity to learn. Nobody has ever written a perfect first draft.

Apply this to others too. Don't savage another writer's work, even if you think it's terrible. Find positive qualities in the writing, if you can, and find a way to suggest areas of improvement without being destructively critical.

Remember that writing anything at all is a huge undertaking. Writing is hard work and everybody struggles with it at times. So whether you are critiquing others' writing or your own, find a way to be encouraging. Focus your criticism on deepening your engagement with the work: Does it say what you really wanted to say? Does it reflect your true voice? How can you improve the work so it's a truer reflection of what you need to say?

Another way to work with this slogan is look at your characters. There may be certain weaknesses that you don't like in yourself or in others, but giving those flaws to your characters will make them appear more rounded. It's the fatal flaw, the insecurities, failure, and weaknesses, that make a character interesting and ultimately drives the story.

Every flaw has a backstory. People are the way they are for a reason. Noticing their flaws and embracing them with compassion can make for better storytelling. And the same applies to you and your flaws.

Exercises

What really gets your goat about other people? Make a list in your slogan journal of all the annoying things you love to criticise in others.

We often criticise others for characteristics and behaviour that hides in our own shadow. Look at your list of criticisms and turn them around. Do you secretly have these characteristics yourself?

What are your flaws and weaknesses? Make a list of the main ones (they might match up with your list of criticisms) but don't beat yourself up about them. Simply recognise them as they are.

Take one of your flaws and tell its story. Don't criticise yourself, but write with compassion and understanding.

Slogan 26: Don't ponder others

This slogan continues from the previous one and is about not making assumptions about what you think might be going on inside another person's head. Even if you're an empath or good at reading people, you could be wrong. There's usually more going on than you can perceive or understand.

The original slogan is the same: *"Don't ponder others,"* and acts as a reminder that you can never know the motivations of others for certain. You will never really know why somebody acts the way they do. The chances are, they don't even know why they do the things they do.

Pondering others is something everybody does. It's a normal part of being human and is how we try to understand each other. But it's also a way to compare yourself with others in order to make yourself feel better. Perhaps you take others apart, looking for faults, and think, *"Well, I'm not as bad as her!"* Or perhaps you deconstruct their actions to figure out where you stand with them, *"She's smiling so that means she must like me!"*

This tendency to act as a mind reader is driven by insecurity, if you have low self-esteem, or is used to boost your sense of superiority, if you're an egomaniac. Either way, pondering others is often more about how you feel about yourself than it is about the other person. You're not that interested in understanding them or developing compassion, you just want to know how to get what you want.

As a mechanism for understanding, it's not very good, but that doesn't stop us from doing it. Our ponderings feed into the social pecking order as we jostle for position by answering questions like: Where do I fit in the group? Who is on my side, who can I trust? Who is my friend and who is my enemy?

You only tend to compare yourself to others and indulge in this kind of inner gossiping with yourself when you feel insecure and cut off from your deeper Self. So this slogan turns it around and says don't ponder others – look at yourself. Look at your motivation for pondering others. Are you really trying to understand and accept others, or are you trying to put them in their place? Are you trying to make yourself feel better?

The more you accept yourself the less likely you are to compare yourself to others in this way. You will never fully understand others, but you can seek to understand yourself better. And the more you understand and accept yourself, the easier you will find it to accept others as they are.

Although this slogan tells you to stop pondering others, that doesn't mean you don't notice when somebody is struggling. It doesn't mean you don't, offer help or advice, if they ask. It's just a reminder that whatever you think is going on, you could be wrong, so have some humility.

For Writers

This slogan seems counterintuitive because writers spend most of their time pondering others. You might even have become a writer because you found pondering others to be such an enjoyable activity!

Pondering others is a major part of a writer's job description. You can't write well, if at all, without pondering others. You have to figure out what your characters are thinking and what their hidden motivations are – that's the whole point of storytelling. So how can you use this slogan without undermining your whole raison d'être?

This slogan can be applied wisely when dealing with criticism of your work, questions about what agents and publishers want from you, as well as market trends and reader reviews.

Not all feedback is equally relevant or useful. When you receive feedback or criticism on your writing, you will need to discern which parts to take on board and which parts you can safely ignore. This is a tricky balancing act, but it's even more difficult if you start trying to deconstruct why somebody has reacted to your work the way they have.

More importantly, don't assume you know why an agent, editor, or publisher has rejected your writing. This is especially hard when you receive a standard rejection that gives you no clues as to why they have said no. It might be because your writing isn't good enough, but it might just be that it's not right for them, or that they liked it but they're looking for something else. The possibilities are endless so don't ponder agents.

As far as market trends are concerned, despite many who will try to convince you otherwise, nobody knows what will sell. If you try to hitch a lift on the latest bandwagon by writing something that fits with current bestsellers, you might succeed, but you might not. Publishing schedules are always slightly behind the marketplace, so you will always be trying to catch up. It's an exhausting way to write, and you're probably better off concentrating on writing something you believe in rather than something that might sell. So don't ponder markets.

Finally, reader reviews are difficult to predict and impossible to control. There really isn't any point in worrying about what others think about your work once it has been published. Of course, you want people to enjoy your writing but you can't control whether they will or not. The only way to stay sane in relation to reader reviews is to ignore them. So don't ponder reviewers.

Exercises

Go to your favourite spot to practice people watching – a café, park, railway station, street corner – and do what you do best: watch people. But this time, do it without coming up with any stories about the people you see – just let the world go by. Watch without pondering and see what happens.

Later, write in your slogan journal about your experience of watching without pondering. Don't retrospectively begin to ponder others! Just write what you noticed, about others and yourself.

Wean yourself off reading your reviews by doing the following:
- Read the bad reviews for a book you thought was brilliant
- Read the good reviews for a book you thought was terrible
- Read both the good and bad reviews for the latest bestseller

Keep doing this until you are thoroughly disillusioned about book reviews.

Slogan 27: Work with your biggest problems first

This slogan is about getting to the heart of whatever holds you back and dealing with that first. When you heal your biggest problems first, the rest will be a walk in the park.

The original slogan is: *"Work with the greatest defilements first."* Defilements seems like a loaded word, full of judgement and condemnation, but it just means anything that gets in the way of you feeling at peace with yourself or accepting yourself as you are. So your greatest problems are your bad habits, negative thinking, emotional complexes, hang ups, fears, doubts, imperfections – anything that stops you being all that you can be and doing what you need to do.

This slogan encourages you to stop avoiding these problems and tackle them head on. These are your real problems. Don't waste time worrying about little niggles and minor upsets because they will heal themselves if you deal with the root of the problem, the thing that never goes away and never seems to get better.

Over time you have probably noticed that the same problems keep coming up in your life. You trip yourself up, over and over, circling around issues you know you should deal with but don't know where to start. This slogan tells you to start with those very problems that you keep avoiding. Whatever you keep putting off or don't know how to deal with or can't face. Begin there.

The things you avoid are often camouflage for other problems. They stack inside each other like Russian Dolls, layer upon layer of hidden motivations and avoidance. So finding your biggest problem may involve some excavation work. You might have to dig down through layers of excuses before you find the real cause of the problem.

For example, you might think you don't have time to meditate on a regular basis and keep putting it off. You use your busy life as an excuse to avoid meditating, but underneath the poor time management may be a fear of change. If you meditate or treat yourself with more kindness, you will start to become somebody else – somebody who likes themselves, somebody who is happy. You may think that's what you want, but perhaps there's another part of you that's frightened because it believes it doesn't deserve to be happy.

In this example, the biggest problem is the lack of self-worth, the belief that you don't deserve to feel happy or be at peace with yourself. So this is what you need to work on with compassion and understanding.

As you make friends with yourself and treat yourself with kindness in small ways, moment by moment, you slowly erode the hold your biggest problems have on your mind. Then the smaller difficulties fall away of their own accord.

For Writers

This slogan encourages you to face one of the biggest stumbling blocks that writers have to deal with: procrastination. Every writer procrastinates, it's probably part of the job description along with people watching. But procrastination can become a real problem if you let it get out of hand.

There is always some tension when you first sit down to write. It's a natural part of the process. You try to turn your mind towards your work, but it bounces away and suddenly you're checking your email (again) or surfing click bait online. With determination you can pull your focus back to the page and begin to write. But sometimes you can't.

Writers procrastinate because writing is hard. It takes a long time to produce work that's even close to acceptable, never mind perfect, so there's a tendency to put it off and do something easier. Knowing this can help you to combat procrastination when it rears its distracting head. But what about those times when you get well and truly stuck?

Chronic procrastination is usually caused by a deeper problem hidden beneath layers of excuses and avoidance. This slogan reminds you to dig down to the roots and find the true cause of whatever it is that stops you from writing. This may change over time. Your biggest problem today may be different to your biggest problem tomorrow, but if you keep digging, eventually you will uncover the one thing that never seems to improve.

When you find this core problem you will need to be honest with yourself about what you're feeling and why you are avoiding it. You can take the edge off by practising tonglen with whatever you discover. Turn towards the fears that block you and breathe out compassion.

This slogan can also be a reminder that your problems are potential goldmines of material for your writing. Whatever you have the most difficulties with, the ideas you're scared to tackle, those are the things you should be writing about. Don't avoid the subjects or feelings that bring you out in a cold sweat or give you vertigo whenever you think of them.

Remember that everybody feels these things; everybody struggles with the same problems you face. If you can find a way to write about your problems, many people will be grateful for your insight. Confronting your own problems will deepen your writing and help you to connect in a meaningful way with your readers.

Exercises

In your slogan journal, make a list of all the ways you procrastinate in order to avoid writing.

When you feel blocked and don't know what to write, write about your frustration, your fear, or your doubt. Write your way through the layers of excuses until you find the root of the problem.

Identify your biggest problem, the thing that always comes up and never seems to improve. Write about the problem in your journal by free writing whatever comes up. Don't censor yourself – just write.

Take your biggest, juiciest problem and create a character and story through which you can explore your feelings and ideas.

Slogan 28: Abandon hope

This slogan is about not being attached to the outcome of whatever you are doing. You might succeed or fail but focusing on either possibility takes you out of the present moment, which is the only time you can act.

The original slogan is: *"Abandon any hope of fruition."* This means abandoning hope of achieving specific results. In relation to mind training, that means you don't hope for enlightenment or any kind of improvement. This seems quite negative on face value. Surely having a goal or something to aim for is a good thing. If you don't believe you can improve, why would you bother trying in the first place?

But this slogan doesn't mean you should give up having goals or doing things to change your life. A sense of purpose and achievable goals can help to keep you motivated, but in reality, you don't know what will happen. You don't know if you will succeed or fail. If you tie your self-esteem or happiness to a particular outcome and it fails to materialise, hope quickly turns to disappointment and disillusionment.

Success is what everybody wants because failure is seen as a bad thing. When you fail it often feels unfair. You might even believe you're a bad person because you failed, or that you didn't deserve to succeed. The hope for success and the fear of failure are internalised as you grow up and condition your approach to everything you do. In fact, hope and fear are joined at the hip – they always arise together. When you focus on a goal in the future, hope and fear will inevitably drive your actions.

But life is unpredictable and uncertain. The future is always unknown. You can fool yourself into believing you know what's going to happen because you believe in the stories you tell yourself about who you think you are and what you think life is about. But the truth is, you have no idea. You only know what you're doing right now.

This slogan tells you to abandon hope but that also means abandoning fear. You have no more reason to despair for the future than you have to hope, because you don't know what will happen. It makes no sense to attach your hopes or fears to something you can't control. You still have to act, but with no guarantee of the outcome, everything you do becomes a leap of faith.

So this slogan is about being focused on the present moment instead of grasping after the future. When you accept the present, it creates a space for you to open to whatever might happen next. It's a way to stay flexible so you can adapt to whatever comes. Abandoning hope doesn't mean turning away from the future or giving up or never having anything to look forward to. As long as you're still alive and breathing you can embrace the present moment, and it's only out of this moment that the future (whatever it may be) will arise. But when it arises, it will be now.

For example, if your goal is to develop self-mastery through mind training so you can feel more peaceful, then the only way to do that is to practice self-mastery right now. It's no good fantasising about how peaceful you'll be in the future. If you want inner peace, you must focus on doing things that bring about that state in the present.

And if you fail to develop inner peace? Keep practising!

For Writers

Issues around success and failure can cause huge problems for writers. Writing well involves a lot of trial and error, and it can take a long time to produce work that meets professional standards. So the experience of failure is built-in to the process of writing. You can't write without failing. Over and over again. But it's that process of failure that helps you learn the craft and eventually produce work that is good enough to succeed.

Fear of failure may drive you to succeed, but you could also feel so scared that you don't even try. In fact, the odds of getting published are stacked against you. Statistically speaking, you are more likely to fail than succeed, but if you think about that and really take it to heart, you will never write a word.

Having said that, hope can also cause problems. Knowing that the odds are unfavourable, you might just cross your fingers and hope for the best. This can lead to passivity and a fatalist approach where you only write things that have a good chance of success. You'll avoid taking risks and rarely stray outside your comfort zone, and your writing may suffer as a result.

You can also run into problems if your writing goals are too rigid. You might get fixated on what you're trying to achieve to the exclusion of everything else in your life. Or become so focused on achieving a goal in a specific way that you don't notice other options that might be open to you.

For example, you might spend years sending a novel out to agents and publishers with the intention of achieving traditional publication believing that this is the only way to get your book into the hands of readers. But the industry might not be looking for that particular kind of book right now, so it might make more sense to self-publish. Or put the novel aside and write something else.

This slogan encourages you to let go of your attachment to the outcome, but you need to be honest with yourself. You could be holding on to a particular outcome without realising it. You might tell yourself that you don't mind whether your book gets published or not, perhaps you're just writing for yourself, for the fun of creating something new. But if every rejection feels like a knife to the chest, it's clear you're still attached to the dream of publication.

Writing is always a leap into the unknown. So abandon hope for publication, fame and fortune. Don't even hope that you will finish your latest project. It may seem crazy to think this way, but to write your best work you must be focused on the present, not the future. When you focus on the present and what you can do right now, it stops you getting caught between the twin fears of success and failure and worrying about things you can't control.

Abandon hope. Let go and write.

Exercises

In your slogan journal, make a list of all your hopes: for your writing, mind training, and life in general.

Now write about what success means to you. Work down your list of hopes and explore how you would feel if you achieved all your dreams.

Identify a writing project that failed. Write about how that failure made you feel and what you learned from the experience.

Identify your ultimate hope, your main dream. Write about how you would feel if you never achieve it. What can you learn from this?

Slogan 29: Don't poison yourself

This slogan is about not feeding your ego with negative or positive reinforcement. The original slogan is: *"Abandon poisonous food,"* which puts the emphasis on how you are nourishing yourself, not just in terms of the food you eat, but on every level: physical, emotional, mental, and spiritual. So don't poison yourself with toxic food, emotions, thoughts, or spiritual practices.

Nourishing yourself is about how you take care of yourself, how you treat yourself with respect and avoid doing things that make your life worse. This might not be obvious because you often don't notice what you're taking in. You might not realise how poisonous something is until the damage has been done.

An obvious example would be food that is contaminated in some way, such as chicken containing salmonella bacteria that gives you food poisoning. Emotions and thoughts can also have hidden impacts or long term effects that you might not notice for a while.

Thinking negatively about yourself is obviously bad for you. Low self-esteem will eat away at your happiness and undermine your ability to take charge of your life over time. But being too quick to congratulate yourself, thinking you're great and can do no wrong, is just as poisonous because it can make you believe you're better than other people. It's a subtle way to put others down.

Negative thinking about yourself reflects fear of what others think about you, and negative thinking about others reflects how you really feel about yourself. Either way, it's all about you. This slogan is saying watch what you think and don't be self-centred. Putting yourself down is as much an ego trip as believing you can do no wrong. So don't poison yourself with thoughts and emotions that don't serve your highest good or stop you from living in a life-affirming way.

That doesn't mean you should start practising positive thinking and fill your mind with affirmations to block out self-doubt. You don't need to deny your problems or how you're feeling. It's not easy to change the way you think and you won't be able to stop poisonous thoughts completely. But this slogan can remind you to pay attention to the way you treat yourself and to let the negativity go.

In the end this practice is about being careful what you feed to your ego. The ego will feast on anything that passes through your mind and experience. It's very good at hijacking whatever you're doing and taking the credit for itself.

Spiritual practices like meditation and compassion are about loosening the grip the ego has on your mind. When your practice is going well, your mind is calm and you feel great. But this is where the ego steps in and starts to feel virtuous. It secretly congratulates itself because it's doing such a great job of meditating. Rather than becoming weaker, the ego gets stronger and you begin to develop what's called a 'spiritual ego.' And the spiritual ego is the greediest of all.

So be careful what you feed your mind.

For Writers

Most writers struggle with self-doubt and negative thinking at some time or another. The process of writing and rewriting and improving your work is impossible without feedback and criticism, and it's easy to become overwhelmed by doubt along the way. This slogan can help to remind you to let go of any negativity that arises as a result of this process.

Your writing won't always go the way you planned. You might spend many hours, months, even years, perfecting a story, only to realise that it simply doesn't work. This doesn't mean you're a bad writer and should immediately give up and find a new hobby.

Writing is a process and you learn along the way. The only way to learn is to make mistakes, to wander down blind alleys, or go around in circles. Every piece of writing that you do will help to make you a better writer if you're determined to learn from your mistakes.

So don't beat yourself up when your writing doesn't turn out as well as you hoped. Don't poison yourself with unnecessary negativity. Instead, see it as an opportunity to learn something and improve your work.

Another way you can poison yourself as a writer is to take too much pride in your work. There's nothing wrong with being proud of the good work you have done and the personal or professional milestones you have achieved. But if you're so proud of your writing that you can't see that it isn't good enough yet and still needs work, then you won't be open to constructive criticism and you won't learn or develop as a writer.

Finally, it's worth remembering that your best work often happens almost by accident. When you're writing well, you get into the zone and the writing feels effortless. There's no resistance or doubt; it just flows out. Later, your ego reads back what has been written and thinks, "*Look what I did! Aren't I fabulous!*" But the ego didn't write it – the writing wrote itself.

This slogan reminds you not to take too much credit for your brilliant ideas and perfect prose. It's not your ego that does the writing. Don't allow it to poison your talent and potential by hijacking your writing. The more your ego is invested in your writing, the harder it will be to relax and enjoy the process of creating new ideas.

Don't poison yourself and don't poison your writing.

Exercises

In your slogan journal, list all the ways you poison yourself: physically, emotionally, mentally, and spiritually.

Identify the poisonous habits, thoughts and feelings that disrupt your writing. Pick one and write about how you can apply an antidote to the poison.

List ten ways you can nourish yourself and your writing.

Slogan 30: Don't be predictable

This slogan is about breaking through your conditioning so you don't react in the same way all the time. The original slogan is more or less the same: *"Don't be so predictable,"* and it draws your attention to your habits of feeling, thought, and behaviour.

Humans are creatures of habit. We like our routines because they make us feel safe and give our lives structure. You know what to expect when you keep doing the same things all the time. Habits make life seem more predictable and controllable. When you do things the same way, day in, day out, you can convince yourself that you know what you're doing and that life is under your control.

But life isn't that controllable. Unexpected things happen all the time and you don't really know what's going on or what you're doing. Your daily habits can hide this fact, so this slogan is prodding you to wake up and pay attention. Don't fall into predictable ways of behaving and thinking.

Some habits can be helpful, while others can become a straightjacket. So the first thing to do is to pay attention to what you're doing and thinking and feeling, and look at the consequences of your habits. Unhelpful habits are the ones that cause you and others to have problems.

You might notice that you have the same automatic responses in certain situations. Perhaps you always get annoyed by the same things, or tend to avoid doing certain things or going to certain places, out of habit, without realising why. These kinds of reactions are usually driven by unconscious emotional conditioning which is often negative and based on fear and the need to protect your ego from perceived, or imagined, threats.

When taken to an extreme, these automatic reactions can lead to serious problems, such as obsessive compulsive disorder, anxiety, and panic attacks. Your life ends up running in ever decreasing circles and it becomes difficult to do anything that isn't defined by your negative habit.

Even when things don't become that extreme, you often drift through your days on autopilot without even realising it. The biggest challenge can be to change the way you think, because even positive habits can become routine and predictable.

For example, when you're practising something like mindfulness or an exercise regime, you can get so used to doing things the same way that you end up going through the motions. It becomes so familiar that you just do it on autopilot. You might start to feel a little bored and begin to think about giving up because it doesn't seem to be doing you any good. But you're only feeling like this because you've fallen asleep at the wheel. You're not paying attention to what you're doing and have fallen into a predictable pattern.

This slogan encourages you to notice your patterns and habits. Pay attention to the way you react and try to catch yourself in the act of reacting. When you notice an automatic reaction, mentally take a step back and ask yourself, "*What am I doing?*"

Don't be so predictable. Switch off the autopilot and fly free.

For Writers

This slogan is about freeing your mind so you don't think or write in the same way all the time. It's easy to fall into predictable habits in your writing, especially when you find a way of writing that works particularly well for you. But breaking out of your habits, good or bad, will help you to express yourself in a more vivid, alive, and spontaneous way.

When you begin a new piece of writing, it can take time to discover what it's really about or what you want to say. Often you don't realise what you need to say until it's written down. This uncertainty can make you feel insecure and doubt your ability to tell the story or complete the work. But it's just part of the process. It's not a sign that you're doing something wrong.

The worst thing you can do is hide from the uncertainty by falling back on old habits, turns of phrase or clichés that you've used before.

This slogan can remind you to pay attention to those times when you're tempted to repeat yourself or avoid taking a risk on something new.

Don't automatically assume you know the best way to write a story, article, or poem. Allow the story to reveal itself in its own way.

This isn't something that only applies to amateurs or aspiring writers. Even when you have been writing for a long time and have completed many stories, each new piece of writing is a fresh beginning. You'll never reach a time when you can confidently say that you know what you're doing. Professional writers don't know what they're doing either.

Another way to apply this slogan is to the idea of whether or not you should plan a story before you write it. Some writers work from detailed outlines and have every twist and turn mapped out; while others jump in and write whatever comes up. They might have a vague idea where they're heading, but the story evolves as they write it.

There isn't a right or wrong way to do this – you have to experiment and see what works for you. The less planning you do, the more spontaneous you'll be, but that doesn't mean the story will be less predictable. You can create a plan for your story that includes unpredictable twists, or a character may unexpectedly say or do something that takes the story off in a totally new direction. You then have to decide whether to go with the character, or rein them in and stick to your original plan.

Whatever you decide to do, if you assume you know what you're doing, the writing will be just like everything else you've ever written. Stale and lifeless.

When you catch yourself getting into a rut with your writing and it's getting stale, do something different. Write in a style you haven't tried before. If you always write in one particular place, go out and change the scenery. If you write on a computer, switch to pen and paper, and vice versa; or write using your non-dominant hand. Or don't write anything – go for a walk.

Whatever you do, don't be predictable.

Exercises

Go for a walk in a neighbourhood you know well but really pay attention to your surroundings. See how many unusual or unexpected things you can find.

In your slogan journal, do writing exercises that force you to be unpredictable, such as writing acrostics, playing word games, picking a random phrase and writing on it for a set time, and so on. Devise your own exercises to flex your unpredictability muscles, or try these:

Create a poem using words and/or phrases cut out of another document, such as a magazine or newspaper.

Use dice or flip a coin to create ideas for a story. Begin by assigning story elements to a number, or heads/tails, then roll the dice or flip the coin to create the structure for your story.

Slogan 31: Don't be mean

This slogan is about not being nasty about other people, either to their face or behind their back. Words can hurt just as much as sticks and stones.

The original slogan is: "*Don't malign others,*" which is a noble idea, but not always easy to live up to. It's no good pretending to be nice on the surface and thinking badly of others in the privacy of your own head. Maligning others when their backs are turned will poison your relationships with everybody. Slogan 29 reminds you not to poison yourself, but it's just as important not to poison others.

Being mean about other people can make you feel better about yourself in the short term. If you feel insecure or uncertain, lashing out may bolster your ego, making it seem larger or more formidable than it really is. This is especially true when you gang up against somebody with a group of friends. Nothing unites people faster than a common enemy. But what kind of person can only feel good by putting others down?

In the end, your attitude towards others will reflect back onto you. A friend might calculate that if you're bitching about somebody else behind their back, you could be doing the same to them. This two-faced attitude erodes trust and creates a bad atmosphere. The truth will come out eventually, and nobody wants to be friends with someone who is always being mean.

This slogan asks you to look more deeply into the intentions behind your words. Why do you say the things you say? What's really behind your attitude towards others?

It's possible to be mean without realising you've done it. You may say the wrong thing and inadvertently upset someone because you were unaware of the significance of your words. You don't know what's going on inside others' heads or what difficulties they may be struggling with, so don't be too quick to judge their behaviour.

When you accidentally say the wrong thing, be honest with yourself and examine your motives. Did you really have innocent intentions? There are many possibilities, and your real motives may be hidden beneath layers of confusion and self-doubt. Are you trying to understand others or do you want to come across as being right or knowledgeable? Do you want to connect and communicate, or are you pushing others away? Do you secretly want others to feel sorry for you?

And what do you do when others are mean to you? This slogan isn't saying you should always be nice. You don't have to benignly accept other people's bad behaviour. There are ways to criticise and help others without being destructive, and it begins with your attitude towards yourself.

Just remember, when you're tempted to snipe, meanness is contagious and what goes around comes around.

For Writers

Writers are not always supportive of other writers. It may be professional jealousy or insecurity and self-doubt, but some of the most vicious critiques of your writing will come from other writers. And then there are the editors and readers.

When you receive negative feedback on your work, it's tempting to hit back and defend your writing as if you're fighting for your life. This is worth remembering when you're in the position to give feedback on other people's work.

Check your motives. Do you really want to help your fellow writers to improve their work, or are you looking for a way to feel superior? Perhaps you want to present yourself as an expert or more experienced, and so deserving of respect or power. You may actually be a better writer and have more experience, but this doesn't give you the right to use that fact to intimidate or undermine the people you're claiming to help.

One of the worst places for this kind of power play is writing groups, whether they meet in person or online. Many groups are supportive and genuinely helpful, but others can harbour bruised egos and resentful hacks looking for an excuse to indulge in malicious gossip and precisely targeted sarcasm. The negative atmosphere may not be overt.

Devastating criticism can be delivered with a smile and a knife to the back.

Nobody can write well in that kind of environment. You can't relax and trust that you will be given a fair hearing if you're scared that every word you write will be savaged.

This slogan reminds you to think before you open your mouth and consider the consequences of your words, as well as the intent behind them. Most people will like and trust you more if you're not being mean.

This applies equally to your online behaviour. If you want to take your writing seriously, you have to consider how you come across when you interact with others. It takes moments to tweet a snarky put-down or to laugh at another's mistake. But a malicious tweet lasts forever. Who will want to work with you or buy your books if you social media feeds are choking with nasty comments and bitchiness?

You need allies in this business. You may write alone, but when it comes to selling your work and finding readers, attitude is everything. Nobody wants to work with an unpleasant grouch.

Words are powerful. Use them wisely.

Exercises

Write a story about a mean person that reveals the hidden reasons for their bad attitude.

In your slogan journal, list all the mean things others have said to you over the years. How did it make you feel?

Take a break from social media for a few days, or even a week, and see if it has an effect on your mood. If you don't use social media, give it a try for a week and see what effect it has on your mood.

Slogan 32: Don't wait in ambush

This slogan is about not holding a grudge or seeking revenge when somebody has hurt you. The original slogan is the same, and is related to the previous slogan about not being mean. When you wait in ambush, you're waiting for an opportunity to be mean, going out of your way to spring an attack or craft the perfect comeback. You wait for somebody to make a mistake or display weakness, and then use it to bait them, laugh at them, or feel smug.

We see this kind of tit for tat behaviour going on every day, especially online. It seems that everybody is enraged about something. The insults fly back and forth, and it can quickly spiral out of control and turn into a screaming match. When this happens, it's impossible to communicate or seek understanding because the people involved have stopped listening to each other.

This slogan reminds you not to seek revenge when somebody has upset you. That doesn't mean you should deny how you feel or ignore what has happened. You need to be honest about your feelings, but retaliation won't make you feel better. It might feel good in the short term, but in the long run, it feeds into your negativity and becomes a vicious cycle.

Grudges can tear families and nations apart, destroy friendships and wreck relationships. When you hold a grudge, the original insult or injury stays with you, lodged in your mind, eating away at you. The need for revenge becomes a poison that infects your mind.

Holding onto anger has the same effect, as this great quote by Buddhaghosa in *The Path of Purification* makes clear. He explains, "*By doing this you are like a man who wants to hit another and picks up a burning ember or excrement in his hand and so first burns himself or makes himself stink.*"

When you do this, it means other people have more control over your own mind than you do. When you hold a grudge or seek revenge you're allowing others to dictate how you feel and think. This is the opposite of freedom and spontaneity and it will never make you happy.

On the other hand, you can't force yourself to forgive someone, especially if their behaviour has caused a lot of suffering. Healing from past hurts takes time and you can't rush it. But this slogan encourages you to take a step in the direction of making peace with others, and your own past.

In the end, an eye for an eye makes everybody blind.

For Writers

It may seem like an obvious thing to say, but not everybody will enjoy your writing. There will be people who just don't understand where you're coming from or aren't interested in the stories you want to write. Sometimes those people will say hurtful things about your work. This slogan reminds you not to seek revenge for bad reviews or negative criticism.

It may be more difficult to deal with destructive editing or the unscrupulous behaviour that can sometimes happen in dark corners of the publishing industry. If you're trying to get published, it's more or less certain that you will get ripped off at some point. There are many predators waiting to take advantage of inexperienced writers so you will need to educate yourself and be careful.

And if the worst happens, don't lash out. If you lose control over your work, or lose money, or your reputation is damaged, there are legitimate ways to deal with it. You don't need to burn down the offending party's office! There are individuals and organisations that can help you gain redress legally.

This slogan also reminds you not to use others' bad behaviour as justification for your own failures. If you do get ripped off, be honest with yourself about your own responsibility for the situation. Did you double-check the details of the contract? Did you take your eye off the ball? Don't blame others for your own mistakes, even if they have mistreated you.

There may be people waiting in ambush to trip you up, but you can also do this to yourself. You might set yourself up to fail by taking on too much or by trying to achieve something beyond your current abilities.

When the inevitable happens, you pounce on the failure and hold it up as evidence for your lack of talent. You wait for yourself to make a mess so you can beat yourself up about it, *"See! I'm an idiot. I can't write. I shouldn't have even tried..."*

In the end, seeking revenge and holding grudges takes up a lot of space in your head. It's much better to fill that space with imagination and new ideas and possibilities. You can't write well if your mind is clogged with resentment and blame. So when you feel like seeking revenge – let it go.

Exercises

In your slogan journal, list all the grudges you are holding, from the silly to the serious.

Pick one of your grudges and write about how it makes you feel.

Write a story of revenge – but with a twist. Show the futility of holding a grudge and the consequences on everybody involved.

Slogan 33: Don't make things painful

This slogan is about not making a bad situation or feeling worse by dwelling on it in a negative way. The original slogan is: *"Don't bring things to a painful point,"* and it follows naturally from the previous slogan about not holding a grudge.

Everybody worries, at times. Either something has already gone wrong, or you're worried about something that might go wrong in the future. Or perhaps both. But when you get caught up thinking negatively about your situation, it makes your problems seem worse. And then it's even harder to stop worrying and find a solution.

When you feel overwhelmed by difficulties it can seem as if you've lost control of your life. Worrying and constantly dwelling on your problems then becomes a way to regain control and understand where you went wrong. Perhaps if you can nail down all the details you'll feel prepared and ready for whatever happens next. But this rarely works. Life will always surprise you with something else.

Some of your problems may be more in your mind than in reality. But even if there are real difficulties with yourself and your situation, going over and over them won't help, and it certainly won't make you feel better. Complaining and brooding about it just makes you feel worse.

When you feel overwhelmed by negativity, ask yourself why. Why are making things so painful? Are you trying to control the uncontrollable? Or perhaps it gives you an excuse to avoid moving towards a solution and actually changing things.

Too much negativity can be discouraging. It undermines your confidence and belief in yourself, and makes it harder to think straight. But you don't have to turn the molehills of your problems into enormous scary mountains in your mind. You can choose to change your mind.

This slogan encourages you to be more positive. Focus on your strengths and the things you do well. This doesn't mean you should avoid thinking about your problems and become a Pollyanna who pretends that everything is fine. Just don't make things more painful than they need to be.

This applies equally to how you deal with other people. If you focus only on their faults and weaknesses, it won't help them to improve. When others cause problems, don't make it worse by humiliating them. Everybody struggles at times and it doesn't always help to focus on what is wrong.

So don't suffer over your suffering. Accept yourself and life as it is, and remember to return to the peace of your true Self. From that still centre in your heart, you can approach every problem with compassion by emphasising the positive without denying the negative.

For Writers

Writing is a process that is beset by failure. It can take a long time, many drafts and many failures, before you find the perfect way to tell a story or the ideal form for a poem. So there will be times when writing is a real struggle and it may seem that you will never get it right.

This slogan reminds you not to beat yourself up when your writing doesn't turn out as you had hoped. You will have good days and bad days. You'll do a lot of bad writing, and sometimes you won't write anything at all. It's all part of the process. Don't listen to the voices in your head that brood over every clunky phrase and crude metaphor. When you're having difficulties with your work it isn't a sign that you should give up or that you can't really write. There's no need to make it more painful than necessary by focusing on the difficulties of the process.

When you receive bad reviews or negative criticism, you can either learn from it or turn it into another stick to beat yourself with. Remember that not all critiques are equally worthy of your attention. Don't make destructive feedback worse by arguing over the details or trying to prove the reviewer wrong.

You can also apply this slogan when you are giving feedback to other writers. It's a tricky balance to strike, but you need to find a way to be encouraging and honest about the problems you find in the work. There's no need to make your criticism personal and don't humiliate somebody because their writing is poor.

If you go out of your way to find fault with a person's work or exaggerate the faults you find, consider how you would feel if somebody did the same to you. How would it feel if you took that kind of attitude towards your own work?

Nobody has ever learned anything from a hatchet job.

Instead, focus on the craft of writing and how the work can be improved. Be specific about why you feel something doesn't work, rather than slating it or dismissing it. And if you don't know why a story doesn't work then you have no business criticising it in the first place.

By not making things painful you leave the door open to the possibility of change and improvement. If something you have written doesn't work, you can always rewrite it.

Exercises

In your slogan journal, write about a time when you were overwhelmed by negativity. Explore your feelings about it and how you overcame the problem.

List five to ten things you really suck at – these can relate to writing or life in general. You may want to include more than ten shortcomings, but try to keep the list as short as possible.

Take your list of shortcomings and find something positive to say about each one. Turn the negativity around and look for how you can improve.

Now make a new list of things you really excel at. Make this list as long as you like and add to it whenever you like.

Slogan 34: Don't pass the buck

This slogan is about taking responsibility for the commitments you have made to yourself and others, and not passing the buck onto somebody else.

The original slogan is: *"Don't transfer the ox's load to the cow,"* in other words, don't transfer your load onto others. It's written like this because the ox is stronger than the cow and can carry a heavier burden. So you are the ox and others are the cows. If you are the strongest in any situation, you should carry what is yours.

This doesn't mean that you don't share your problems or seek support when you are struggling. If you're not strong and you need help, then you should ask for it. There's probably an ox around somewhere who will share your burden.

But if you are strong, this slogan encourages you to be honest with yourself. Look at your strengths and weaknesses and how you are responding to the challenges in your life. Are you dealing with your own problems, or are you offloading them onto somebody else? A strong person doesn't dump their emotional problems on others and expect them to deal with it for them.

There may be times when you would prefer to avoid taking responsibility for something, especially if it involves some kind of burden or obligation. For example, when you're a member of a group that's looking for a leader or for individuals to contribute or help in some way, how do you respond?

Do you look at your shoes or pretend you're too busy to help? Do you hide your strengths and talents in the hope that nobody will ask you to step up and put them to the test?

Be honest about what you can do, but also realistic. If you are capable of doing something and you're tempted to dodge the responsibility, this slogan reminds you not to cop out. But you also need to be realistic about what you can and can't manage at any given time.

You don't have to take on so many responsibilities that you can't cope and feel overwhelmed. There's no need to make things worse for yourself, even if you are strong. You need to make wise choices about how you manage your life, what to take on and which burdens to share with others.

You must carry your own load and deal with your own problems. It's your life, after all, and if you don't do the emotional work to understand yourself and make the most of the opportunities that life provides, you only have yourself to blame.

For Writers

This slogan is a kick in the pants.

If you're not writing, but you want to write, then only you can fix the problem. Only you can choose to write. You are responsible for making sure that you live up to your commitments. So if you want to write, you can't blame others when you don't write.

You might have a great idea for a novel, for example, but never find the time to actually sit down and do the writing. Perhaps if you had more time, you would write the book. Or if you didn't have to work at your day job, or raise your kids, and so on. But these are just excuses.

When you find yourself blaming other things for getting in the way of your writing, have a closer look at what you're really saying. Do other people really have more control over your life than you?

It's not your children's fault that you don't write. It's not your job that stops you from focusing on the story ideas in your head. It's not the lack of time. It's you.

Don't pass the buck onto others. You are responsible for the choices you make.

This slogan encourages you to look into why you pass the buck. Why are you making these excuses? Perhaps it's a fear of failure, or of putting your ideas to the test. What if you spend all that time writing and then discover you can't do it, or that you have no talent. Maybe people will laugh at you for even trying.

Or perhaps it's a fear of success. What if you can write and you do really well, and then you have to live up to that success and keep coming up with ideas. People will scrutinise everything you write, and you'll be held accountable.

Only you can confront these fears and doubts, and only you can answer the questions they pose. Don't blame others for your lack of focus, discipline, talent, patience, or confidence. You are the only person who can choose to let go of whatever gets in the way of your writing.

This slogan encourages you to carry the burden of your choices. You must take responsibility for doing whatever you need to do in order to write. Perhaps you need to learn new skills or delegate some of your other responsibilities. If you think your writing isn't good enough, attend a workshop or find a writing group that will help you to improve. If you struggle to organise your complicated life, learn about time management, or simplify your life.

When you do have some success, you're still responsible for carrying your own load. Don't pass the buck onto your agent or publisher in the belief that it's up to them to ensure your books are marketed effectively. You will need to be an active partner in the business of selling your own work.

For more thoughts on taking responsibility, refer back to Slogan 12.

Exercises

In your slogan journal, list all the excuses you have used to avoid writing.

Take one or two of the worst excuses on your list and deconstruct them. What is really going on? What are you avoiding?

Do you hide your talent or strengths, and if so, why? Think of a time when you could have taken responsibility but you hung back. Write about the feelings you had and the reasons you used for passing the buck.

Slogan 35: Don't compete with others

This slogan is about remembering that life isn't a race. You don't have to be the first or the best, and you don't have to compete to win.

The original slogan is: *"Don't try to be the fastest."* Life seems to be getting faster and faster every day. You race against the clock to meet your deadlines at work so you can race home to bolt your dinner and then hit the bars with your friends so you can drink as much as possible and have the best time ever!

Competitiveness is built-in to the way society works, with everyone jostling for position. Everybody wants to be first. Nobody wants to be last. Even having fun becomes a competition. If you slow down you might miss something cool or important. You try to keep up with the frenetic pace, but end up running in circles.

Racing forward into the future like this is all about the destination or the prize. But when you finally get to the pot of gold at the end of the rainbow (if you get there at all), you're too burnt out and exhausted to enjoy it. You can hardly remember the journey you have just taken – it passed in a blur.

Mind training and meditation don't respond well to this competitive approach. You can't meditate faster than others. You could meditate for longer, but what does that prove? Meditation isn't about proving how calm or together you are. It's not about being 'more spiritual' than others or winning an enlightenment trophy for being a saint.

In fact, the harder you push yourself to become calm or peaceful, or to clear your mind of all thoughts, or become more selfless, the less likely you are to actually achieve any of those things. You can't force yourself to relax. Meditation and mindfulness take practice and time, and results will come in their own way and in their own time.

So this slogan is a reminder to slow down. You don't have to compare yourself with others to see how far you have come or still have left to go. Meditation and awakening to your true Self is about how you relate to your inner life. You can't free your mind and find inner stillness if you're always trying to get somewhere or achieve something.

When you stop competing with others it allows you to come home to the present moment. What matters is how you are right now, not how you might be at some point in the future. If you want to be calm in the future, then you have to practice being calm now because that is the only time in which you can actually be present.

Let other people be whoever they are. Then you are free to be you. Slow down, relax and smell the roses.

For Writers

Looking at the bestseller charts for the latest novels makes it hard to believe that writing isn't a competition. Book prizes and awards pit writers against each other and compare novels that often have very little in common. Each book should stand or fall on its own merits, but in the end, one will be declared the winner.

Prizes matter because the marketplace for books is incredibly competitive and many novels struggle to achieve visibility, let alone decent sales. Most writers can't earn a living from their writing and rely on other sources of income to pay their bills. This economic reality and the competitive nature of society puts a lot of pressure on writers to join the race. If you don't write the right kind of book – one that will sell as many copies as possible – you will be left behind. You will lose the race and nobody will read your work.

When you take this approach, it turns writing into a popularity contest. But since everybody has a different opinion about what makes a book good, it's almost impossible to predict which books will sell and which ones will go unloved.

What's a writer to do? You could self-publish your writing, if nobody else will, but you'll still have the same problems of visibility and competing sales. Some people are better at managing this situation than others, and they tend to be the ones who do well. But it still reduces the process of writing to a popularity contest where the winner is the one who shouts the loudest.

Regardless how you feel about this problem, if you want to write a good book – and by that I mean a book that you're proud of and that you're happy to put your name on – you will need to focus on your book. Not other people's books. Yours.

Other writers can't write your book. Only you can write your book. You're not really in competition with other writers because they can't write in your voice. Another writer won't come up with the same story ideas as you – they may think of something similar, but the spin they give the story will be different.

Your voice as a writer is unique. Nobody writes like you. So don't compare yourself to others. Focus on expressing your unique take on life.

If you want to sell your writing, you will have to deal with the marketplace. But it's not a good idea to think about that while you're writing the book. If you compare your writing to others and worry about whether it's acceptable or saleable, you will lose track of your voice.

When you worry too much what others think, it distorts your writing and you end up with a piece of work that falls short of what you may be capable of. Putting other people's opinions ahead of your own almost guarantees that nobody will like what you write – not even you.

To write a book that others will want to read and enjoy, you must be present at every step of the way. Being a writer isn't about selling more, or being more popular, getting better reviews, or even being a better writer than others. Writing is about the process.

Everybody writes in their own way and at their own speed. Some writers manage to publish several books a year, while others take ten years to write one. Some writers write 2,000 words a day, or more. You may only manage 500 words, or less. But that's okay. It's not a race.

So slow down and pay attention to what you're doing. Enjoy the process of writing, and if your story turns out as well as you secretly hope, it will be worth the wait.

Exercises

Identify other writers with a similar style to your own. Why do you admire their work? How is your voice different to theirs?

In your slogan journal, write for ten minutes about any subject of your choice but try to write as much as you can. Really push yourself to write as fast as possible.

Now write another piece, but this time you have as long as you like to finish it. Aim to write about 500 words and take your time – there's no rush.

Compare the two pieces of writing. Is there any difference in quality or voice? How did you feel doing each piece? Maybe writing fast made you feel stressed and pressured. Or perhaps writing fast is your preferred style and you struggled to slow down.

Slogan 36: Don't be sneaky

This slogan is about being honest with yourself about your real motives. The original slogan is: *"Don't act with a twist,"* which means not doing things just to get something out of it for yourself.

When you act with a twist there's an ulterior motive behind your actions. No matter how you appear on the surface, underneath you secretly want to benefit yourself. This is because the ego sees itself as the centre of the universe – it's all about me! But really, it feels insecure so is always looking for ways to make itself appear better, stronger, happier, and so on. Your ego wants others to see you a certain way and will do whatever is necessary to achieve that.

So this slogan tells you not to lie to yourself, or others, about what you're really doing and feeling. If you're being selfish, be honest about it. Don't deceive yourself about your motives. Don't sneak around and use others so you can feel better about yourself.

This kind of manipulative behaviour can be quite subtle and you might not realise you're doing it. Self-deception is one of the hardest things to change because human beings are so good at it! We hide from the truth at the same time as claiming we want to know the truth. We say we want to be free and happy, and then behave in ways that make us feel worse.

Even meditation and mindfulness can be turned into something that secretly boosts your ego. You can become stress free, healthier and happier, just by sitting for thirty minutes a day and not thinking (or trying not to think). It's a wonderful self-improvement exercise, but the underlying motivation is to create a better version of you. The ego loves this and will happily go along with it.

But this isn't what meditation is really about. Spiritual practices like mindfulness and mind training are designed to undermine the ego and reduce its grip on your mind. In the end, it's not really about you, in the sense of your ego feeling better. It's about transcending the need to identify with the ego in the first place.

'Being spiritual' can also backfire through false modesty, where you hide your talents and gifts because you don't want to appear too egotistical. Or perhaps you become excessively virtuous, and your purity acts as a silent judgement of others. If you're too nice and good and perfect all the time, it begins to look like you're trying too hard. The ego sneaks in the backdoor and all that perfection turns to smugness.

Being nice so that others will like you is manipulative and dishonest, and it doesn't fool anyone. Your ulterior motives will backfire eventually, so you may as well be honest.

For Writers

It appears that everybody is trying to sell something these days. Advice for writers often puts a lot of emphasis on how to sell your work, improve your marketing, reach more readers, and become a wiz at networking. It can be tempting to act the way others expect you to in order to get something you want, like a book deal, an agent, or to make a sale.

But this is manipulative and most people can spot a phony a mile off (remember Slogan 24). When you put selling ahead of everything else, you run the risk of becoming a marketeer, the pejorative version of marketer. If you do that, every communication is distorted into a pitch and the hard sell and upselling take over. It becomes all about you and your product or service.

Many people feel conned by these tactics. Nobody wants to spend all their time interacting with people who are relentlessly trying to sell them things, especially things they don't even want. As a writer, it can be hard to work out how to spread the word about your writing without falling into this trap.

You will need to be honest with yourself about your motives and think about why you are writing in the first place. Do you want to sell millions of books? Or do you want to write for the sake of writing? Even if your intention is to sell as many books as possible, you still have to write them.

But when you put selling first it distorts how you see the story and will change how it's written. Doing this gives too much power over to the marketplace to decide which stories should be told and which voices should be heard. Thinking of the market first and the story second puts the cart before the horse, and you won't get far doing that. It reduces writing to a competition and a shouting match, as we saw in Slogan 35.

Once you have written your book, you will have to decide what to do with it and how to sell it without compromising your principles or your voice. How do you share your writing without being sneaky?

Many writers use social networking and blogs to spread the word about their work, but it's not that simple. Nobody goes on Twitter to buy books. People use social media to connect with friends, chat with strangers, and share silly memes. They want real relationships and connections with real people. They don't want people selling them stuff all the time.

So when you use social media as a writer, remember to not be sneaky. Don't have an ulterior motive for networking with others. This applies just as much to networking you do in person at events such as writing conferences or book festivals. Network for the fun of it and to meet people, not to get something out of it or to sell your work.

When you share your work, see it as an outpouring of your creativity and ideas, not as an opportunity to make a quick buck. You can't control how others respond to your work and trying to manipulate them into responding the way you want will backfire. You can share your writing whether people respond or not, whether they buy your books or not.

However you approach the problem, your priority is to write the best book you can write. Remember that you are a writer first and a bookseller second. Don't become a marketeer.

Exercises

In your slogan journal, explore how you feel about selling your writing. How does it make you feel? How do you feel when others try to sell things to you?

Buy a book – or get a book you bought recently.

In your slogan journal, analyse why you bought this particular book. Why were you drawn to it? What interests you about it? Why do you want to read it?

Look at the marketing material for the book you just bought and analyse why you think it works. How did you become aware of the book? Did you feel manipulated by the marketing? Does that matter? What can you learn from your experience buying the book?

Slogan 37: Don't make gods into demons

This slogan is about not using spiritual teachings and practices to feed your ego. The original slogan is the same and it means don't take something good and turn it into something bad. Don't take the best things in your life and turn them into the worst by abusing them or taking them for granted.

When you first begin to meditate it can feel great. You start to notice how much better you feel – you're more relaxed and focused, and the things that used to bother you, don't seem to matter anymore. You feel more comfortable in your own skin and life doesn't seem so scary.

The danger is that you enjoy this newfound ease and openness so much that you settle into being comfortable and stop challenging yourself to face things that make you feel uncomfortable. You end up hiding from yourself inside the practice, which works as long as it feels good. But as soon as something difficult comes up, you quit, or search for a new practice that you can hide inside.

Maybe you start taking meditation for granted, or talk about doing it but never practice, or don't allow what you're learning to really penetrate and change you on a deep level.

Spiritual practice is about transformation and that isn't always easy or comfortable. As your meditation progresses, you slowly learn to break out of the ego cage in your mind. Spiritual teachings and practices soften you up and open your heart, which means you might start feeling things more deeply. But you're not supposed to use the teachings and practices to build a more comfortable cage so you can hide from the things in life that you don't like because they hurt.

Another way you can turn gods into demons is to use spiritual practice as a stick to beat yourself with. Because these practices are about transformation, it's easy to get so focused on improving yourself and trying to become a better person that you end up fixated on how bad you are. Every time you sit down to meditate you notice how crazy your mind is and it just makes you feel worse. You become even more critical and self-flagellating.

But freeing your mind and returning to the peace of your true Self isn't about pointing out all your flaws and problems. It's not about beating yourself up when you get it wrong. If you're suffering, it's not because you're being punished for being a bad person. Hellfire and brimstone only exist in your head.

True spiritual practice is about self-acceptance and making peace with yourself and the world. Just do your best and don't worry when you have a bad day. Notice where you've gone wrong and then let it go. Remember Slogan 33 and don't suffer over your suffering.

This slogan works the other way around too: don't turn demons into gods. Don't take something that really isn't that important or good for you and make it the centre of your life. Don't let something like an addiction or a fear become what drives your choices. Don't let your ego run the show.

For Writers

Who are your writing gods? We all have our favourite authors and writers whose work we admire. There's nothing wrong with this, as far as it goes, but too much hero worship can become a problem.

When you worship another writer's work, you put them on a pedestal. They become an untouchable, unreachable genius. How could you ever hope to write that well? You might even convince yourself to give up writing altogether, since it's such an impossible, hopeless dream. You'll never be able to live up to that level of incandescent talent.

When you turn your writing heroes into gods, you back yourself into a corner. You may struggle to come up with ideas that you think are good enough or creative enough. Or you assume your story idea has already been done, and others have written it so much better than you could. How could you possibly improve on it?

But none of this has any basis in reality. When you read a published novel, you're reading the product of a long period of writing and rewriting and editing and more rewriting. The book may have been taken apart and put back together again, line by line. You have no idea how much work has gone into an apparently perfect book.

Nobody has ever written a perfect first draft. Not even the best writers can pull that off. Not even the genius ones. So don't turn your writing gods into demons of self-doubt. If your first effort at writing a novel is a bit lacklustre, you can rewrite it. You can rewrite it as many times as it takes, and there are no rules on how long that is. (It's generally as long as a piece of string.)

There's another group of people that writers can sometimes elevate above their station: agents and publishers. Every year, agents and publishers claim they are looking for a particular kind of book or a particular kind of writing. They try to predict what the market will want in several years time, and sometimes they get it right. But mostly, they don't.

This is because, in the famous words of screenwriter William Goldman, *"Nobody knows anything."* Agents and publishers have to claim that they know what sells because that is their job. But they usually end up running to catch the trends that happen while nobody is looking, or while everybody is busy pretending to know what they're talking about.

So don't give too much importance to the opinion of agents and publishers. Concentrate on writing the stories you want to write, and write them as well as you can. Because in reality, that is what everybody wants: a good story.

The best writers – your writing gods – are the ones who know how to tell a good story. If you learn anything from them at all, let it be this: As a writer, your only god is the story you are telling.

So do your best. Let go of your mistakes. And keep writing.

Exercises

In your slogan journal, list your favourite authors.

Pick your top three favourite authors and write about why you admire their work. What can you learn from them?

Do some research: What are the latest trends in publishing? What do you think will be selling in five years time? Why? How do you know this?

Slogan 38: Don't profit from another's loss

This slogan is about not exploiting others in order to make yourself happy or successful. The original slogan is: *"Don't seek others' pain as the limbs of your own happiness,"* which means you should avoid seeking to gain from others' loss and suffering.

This can be a difficult slogan to live up to because you might not realise how your good fortune affects other people. In our commercially driven culture, when you win it means somebody else has to lose and this can lead to exploitation.

Society is built on exploitation. The way our lives are structured means that the problems of winning and losing are hard to avoid. If you want to buy cheap clothes, somebody working in a sweatshop on slave wages will probably make them. If you want cheap food, it will be grown using industrial farming methods that are routinely cruel to animals and damaging to the environment.

The hierarchical shape of society, where the rich few at the top exploit the mass of the poor at the bottom, extends down to include the animals and plants, the oceans and the air. The entire earth is exploited as we plunder its resources to enrich ourselves.

It's impossible to live without some level of exploitation – you have to eat something. But most of the time, we live in a way that insulates us from the awareness of that exploitation. You might not be personally exploiting others to get what you want, but the consequences of your choices mean that exploitation happens whether you intend it or not.

This slogan asks you to look at your choices and behaviour to see how much you are taking advantage of others in order to benefit yourself. You can do your best to limit the amount of exploitation in your life and aim to treat everybody as fairly as possible. This can be a challenge because the ego has a strong need to protect itself from threats because it feels insecure. You end up feeling as if you're pitted against the world in a battle for survival – if you lose, you die.

This is a brutal worldview. You can't build your happiness on such a perspective. If your happiness depends on the suffering of others, you end up with a divided world built on exploitation, and nobody can thrive in a world like that.

Real happiness can only come from within. If it depends on external conditions then it's not real because it can be taken away or lost. Real happiness can only arise when everybody is free to be who they are, without fear of exploitation or suffering.

This slogan encourages you not to indulge your ego or get your own back on others when they hurt you. And don't celebrate when others lose, even if you think they deserve it. There's no need to rub salt into their wounds. Everybody suffers and compassion is universal. Think of all the times you have lost while others have won and remember how that feels.

If you want to be happy, you must allow others to be happy too.

For Writers

This slogan brings up the question of exploitation in your writing, and asks you to look at whether there is anything that is off-limits in terms of what you are willing to write about.

Many writers take inspiration from the people they know in order to create characters for their stories. Family members and friends, and especially enemies, can all be used as templates for characters, and even storylines. You might use their basic traits and idiosyncrasies to build a foundation and then flesh the character out with your imagination. Or take somebody you know in their entirety and insert them into your story.

There are many possibilities but they all raise the question of where you draw the line. How much detail do you include? Should you disguise the identities of your inspiration and let them keep their privacy and dignity? How you answer these questions depends on the stories you are writing and how you are using your characters.

Sometimes writers change the names of the people they're using as inspiration, but it's still possible to tell who they're writing about because the characterisation is so vivid. Whereas others will disguise the source of their inspiration so well that you might not realise who a character is based upon, even if you know the person well.

This slogan also encourages you to consider your motives in writing about a particular person or situation. If you're fictionalising something that you have lived through, you will need to think about the effect this will have on the other people involved. What are you trying to achieve by writing about your experience?

Do you want to tell the truth about how it felt to go through the experience? Or are you trying to get back at the people who have hurt you by writing about them? Even if you're not trying to hurt anybody, should you publish the story if it will hurt someone else? Is there a way of writing the story without humiliating them?

These are not easy questions to answer and every story you write may need a different approach. This slogan reminds you to think twice before gleefully destroying somebody (on the page) who has hurt you. Think about how you would feel if someone wrote about you in a way that was hurtful or damaging.

There are ways to write about people, even the ones you don't like, without being wilfully exploitative or mean. Consider this, from Thich Nhat Hanh:

> "When writing a book or an article, we know that our words will affect many people. We do not have the right just to express our own suffering if it brings suffering to others. Many books, poems, and songs take away our faith in life... Writers need to practice Right Speech to help our society move again in the direction of peace, joy, and faith in the future."

Exercises

In your slogan journal, explore whether there are any subjects that are off-limits to you. What will you never write about?

Do you disguise the identities of the people who inspire your work? If so, why? If not, why not?

Who inspires your characters? Analyse your stories and see if you can identify the people you were inspired by.

Slogan 39: Have a single intention

This slogan is about remembering to focus on benefiting others by training in meditation and compassion. You're not here to get something for yourself – you're here to wake up.

The original slogan is: *"All activities should be done with one intention."* This one intention is what underlies all your feelings, thoughts, and behaviour through the day. No matter what you're doing, look at what is going on in the back of your mind and ask yourself: **What do I really want?**

This is relatively easy when you're not too busy, but when life gets hectic you can lose touch with why you're doing things and can end up doing a lot of stuff you don't really need to do. You rush about, juggling your various responsibilities and tasks, and rarely stop to think about why you're doing so much.

Underneath all this busyness there is often a feeling that you're constantly rushing to meet the future – to get something, achieve something, or perhaps finish everything so you can finally stop and relax and do nothing. You're rarely present in what you're doing because you're too busy thinking about the next thing on the list.

So this slogan reminds you to pay attention to what you're doing and why. The idea is to let go of your ego and consider the possibility that you might be here for something other than yourself. Are you here to make money and achieve things that can be lost, such as status, power, and success?

Or are you here to wake up to your true nature?

This slogan reminds you that the purpose of mind training and meditation is to be present. When you focus on the present moment and do things mindfully, you begin to notice that there is no self that is 'doing' anything. Everything arises in a kind of spacious openness that is always present.

This is your true nature, which you share with everyone. So the idea of doing things purely for yourself becomes rather silly because there is no separate self.

Everything you do can be done with the intention to wake up to this truth. No matter what you do, think, or feel, it happens in your awareness, so everything can serve as a reminder of who you really are. Then every act becomes an act of grace and a recognition that you are connected to everyone.

When you have a single intention, everything you do is an expression of your true nature in action – which is what it really means to live for the benefit of others.

For Writers

You can't write effectively if your attention is scattered all over the place. When you're busy or trying to do too many things at once, it fragments your thought process and makes it hard to concentrate. So having a single intention means doing one thing at a time.

Don't have Facebook or Twitter on in the background while you're working and don't allow yourself to become distracted. Pay attention to what you are doing and be present for every word that you write. This will help you to go deeper into the moment, which will bring your writing to life.

And this brings us to an important question: **Why do you write?**

Writers write for many reasons: Self-expression, self-obsession, to explore and understand, to communicate and connect, to feel alive, to make sense of the world and the meaning of life, and even for fame and money, although these are unlikely to materialise.

Maybe you're driven by your obsessions and write about the things that keep you awake at night, the dilemmas you can't resolve and the ideas you'll never fully understand. Maybe you write because it's better than not writing. You don't feel like yourself when you're not spinning a yarn.

Whether it's blind egomania or a desire to transcend the conditioning that makes you crazy, perhaps writing has something to do with the Promethean impulse towards increased consciousness and self-knowledge. Or maybe it's just about having fun.

Stephen King says that ultimately, writing is about *"enriching the lives of those who will read your work, and enriching your own life, as well...It's about getting up, getting well, and getting over. Getting happy, okay? Getting happy."*

This slogan reminds you to pay attention to why you are writing. There are no right or wrong reasons, but if you write because you want admiration, money, and unending glory, be aware that you are likely to be disappointed.

In the end, the best way to get the most out of your writing is to get yourself out of the way. This doesn't mean that you should only write for others and not for yourself. When people talk about writing for others, they usually mean you should give readers what they want. In other words, you write for the market. The only problem with this approach is that other people don't really know what they want. Not specifically.

What readers want from writers is the same thing that writers want from the process of writing. Everybody lives inside their own story. You know things about yourself that nobody else will ever know. You see the world in a way that nobody else could ever imagine. But this means it feels lonely inside your skull.

Writing turns your mind inside out. It's a way to meet yourself coming back in the other direction with recognition and compassion. It reminds you that you're not really alone. And this is what readers want from you too.

When you let go of your ego, you come home to the reality of who you are. You remember that it's not really about you and this creates a space where the story can write itself. And there's nothing more fun than that.

Exercises

In your slogan journal, list all your reasons for writing.

Explore your reasons by analysing your writing process. How does writing make you feel? How do you feel when you don't write? What draws you to a particular story idea or character?

156 FREE YOUR PEN

List some of your favourite books, novels and non-fiction.

Why did you read these books? Don't say, *"Because they're good!"* Dig deeper into your motivation and thought process. Why are they your favourites? What do you think motivated the author to write each book?

Slogan 40: Remember your intention

This slogan follows from the previous one and asks you to remember your intention to be present and to let go of your ego. The original slogan is: "*Correct all wrongs with one intention,*" the 'wrongs' being when you fail to live up to your intention to awaken or feel stuck in your meditation practice.

Being present is difficult and it's easy to get sidetracked. No matter how good your intentions, there will be times when you just can't manage to stay present. Life doesn't always go to plan and there are many ways you can fall off the path and sink back into self-absorption and distraction.

These 'wrongs' are either external or internal. External difficulties can be anything that trips you up on the path, such as unexpected problems, relationship and job upsets, illness and health crises, or just plain old busyness – too much to do and not enough time.

Internal difficulties can be the whole range of your usual emotional problems, self-doubt and confusion about the path you're on, and the challenges of the awakening process itself, such as the dark night of the soul.

When you get stuck like this, you feel frustrated and annoyed with yourself. You want to wake up and feel freer and happier, but it's as if you're going in circles. One day you have a great meditation experience and life feels fantastic, and then the next, your mind is full of fear or anger or confusion and you wonder if you'll ever wake up.

This slogan says that no matter what the problem, you can fix it with one simple intention – the intention to wake up and be present. So even when you're struggling and you feel like you have lost your way, you haven't. The difficulties are part of the path and everything can be used to wake you up.

The fact that you notice the problem in the first place is a sign that you are paying attention. You know something isn't right. You can feel it when you slip up and drift away from the present. All you have to do is notice that this has happened, and then let it go and return to the present moment.

If you get really caught up in a problem, you might need to spend some time looking into it so you can dissolve the negativity and recommit to your intention. Take the problem that has arisen and hold it in your attention, turn it around and investigate where it's coming from and why. Perhaps you need to take a break and stop trying so hard.

Mind training means having the discipline to work with whatever comes up in every moment. Work with the feelings that are causing the problem rather than trying to avoid them or pretend that they're not there. Confusion, fear, anger, and so on, arise because you're not awake. This slogan reminds you that the presence of these feelings is like an alarm clock trying to wake you up.

Every moment is a fresh opportunity to remember who you are and to live for the benefit of others. Time to wake up.

For Writers

There are times when remembering to write is the last thing on your mind. Life is full of so many other problems and distractions, that your desire to write slips to the bottom of a very long list of all the other things you need to do. Unless you prioritise your writing and move it to the top of the list, you may never get round to it. Your idea for that brilliant novel or epic poem will slowly fade from your mind, buried under an avalanche of daily busyness and responsibilities.

Eventually you might even convince yourself that you're not really a writer. Or when you do manage to sit down to write something, nothing happens. You stare at the blank page and feel stupid, inadequate, ridiculous.

This slogan can help you to remember your intention to write every day. No matter what else is going on in your life, if you want to commit to your writing, you must make space for it. Put it on your to do list – at the top.

When you feel stuck and don't know what to write, this slogan encourages you to use whatever is present in your life, right at this moment, to get you writing again. If the blank page feels intimidating or you think you have nothing to say, just write about the room you're sitting in. Or write about how you're feeling. Explore your stuckness, your fear or confusion.

Don't use not knowing what to write as an excuse to not write. Investigate why you're avoiding your writing – and write about it. You either want to write or you don't. There really is no excuse!

Another way to work with this slogan is to explore the idea of wanting to benefit others through your writing. This could mean doing your best to write a good story, one that is well crafted, entertaining and meaningful. Or it could mean sharing your knowledge and experience with others.

It could also mean taking the time to improve your writing to make it easier to read and understand. To benefit others, write in a way that is accessible and don't make your readers work too hard to figure out what you're trying to say. That doesn't mean you should dumb it down or only tell people what they want to hear. There are ways to express complex ideas without being obscure, and you can explore difficult emotions or subjects with sensitivity and respect. You don't have to pull your punches.

Writing with honesty and compassion means telling the truth. What 'truth' is can be interpreted in many different ways, but within the context of the spiritual path we're exploring in this book, it means the reality of this moment – here and now. You can use your writing to explore this moment. Tell the truth of who you are right now and watch your mind in the act of creating the present.

Perhaps the truth will set you free.

Exercises

Prioritise your writing. Take a realistic look at your daily schedule and find a way to move writing closer to the top of your to do list.

Stop reading this and pay attention to the moment. What is happening right now? Grab your slogan journal and capture this moment in words.

In your slogan journal, explore the ways you can benefit others through your writing. Do you benefit others now? If so, how? If not, how could you change this?

Slogan 41: Renew your commitment each day

This slogan is about making an intention to be present every day. The original slogan is: *"Two activities: one at the beginning, one at the end,"* which asks you to make a dedication to be present at the start of the day, and then again at the end.

Every day is a fresh start. No matter what happened yesterday, even if you completely lost the plot, you can always start again today. This applies to every moment too. If you're having a bad day, you can take a breath, clear your mind and make a commitment to start again.

In the morning when you first get up, renew your commitment to your practice – to mind training, meditation, waking up, being more compassionate, kinder, whatever it is that you're trying to achieve. First thing in the morning is a good time to get into a new routine and commit to a positive intention because it sets you up for the day. No matter how the day goes from then on, you're focused on your intention.

You might like to actually state your intention out loud or perhaps incorporate it into your daily meditation practice. Either say or mentally think to yourself something like: *"May I be present,"* or *"May my actions be of benefit to others."* You can use your own words and make an intention that means something to you. Or you could try this simple prayer that is based on the **Four Immeasurables** (see the glossary for the full dedication):

May I be well
May I be happy
May I be free from suffering

May all beings be well
May all beings be happy
May all beings be free from suffering

You may also like to focus your commitment specifically on your mind training practice with the slogans. So your intention could be, *"May I practice lojong with an open heart and mind,"* and then pick a slogan to work with that day.

At the end of the day before going to sleep, review your day to see how it went. Did you keep your intention? Did you manage to stay present and mindful? If you lost focus, why did that happen? You might like to write about your experience in a journal, with the focus on what has benefited others.

Don't beat yourself up if you had a bad day. Just notice where you went wrong and renew your commitment to try again tomorrow. You won't get it right all the time, but that's okay. You don't have to be perfect – just do your best.

Practising this slogan regularly can completely change your life because it will subtly shift how you think about yourself and why you do things. Even one moment of clarity and mindful presence in an otherwise hectic day will make a difference, to yourself and to others.

For Writers

Maintaining momentum and focus in your writing practice can be a challenge, even on a good day. You get distracted or sidetracked and then can't find your way back. If you lose focus for long enough, you may start to doubt yourself and think you're wasting your time trying to write because it feels like you're not getting anywhere. Or worse, going round in circles. You might get so stuck that you stop writing altogether.

If you are a writer then writing is an essential part of your life. That may seem like an obvious statement, but if you don't acknowledge the importance of your writing practice you can't expect to make the most of it. When you don't respect your need to write, you allow other parts of your life to encroach on your writing time, you dismiss creative ideas before they have a chance to take root, and you allow doubt to cripple your motivation and self-belief.

If you want to write then you need to make space for it in your life and treat the process of writing with the respect it deserves. When you make a commitment to your writing, you're making a statement to yourself that this activity is important, that you will give it time and energy and love.

So this slogan encourages you to renew your commitment to your writing practice every day. Doing this will help you to stick to your writing goals and encourage you when you lose focus or have doubts.

If you really want to write, you'll find a way to make it happen. But don't take it for granted that you will write – actually make a statement to that effect. When you get up in the morning, say or think to yourself, *"I will write today."* If you want to make sure you really get the message, say, *"I will write today because I care about my writing."*

Commit to writing something every day, even if it's just a few words or for a short period of time. You'll be surprised by how much you can accomplish writing in short bursts every day. All those sentences and paragraphs add up. And if you didn't write yesterday, don't let it stop you writing today.

To get into a routine and establish a pattern, you might like to practice morning pages. This is just free writing that you do as soon as you get up. Write by hand, about anything you like. Don't think, don't worry about punctuation, spelling or grammar, just let the words pour out in a stream of consciousness.

This is a good way to clear the junk and clutter out of your head, vent your worries and rage, and write your way down into your true voice. If you have a particular story or idea that you want to work on, you can write about that too. Either way, writing first thing in the morning can be a good way to access the creative part of your mind before the rest of it wakes up and takes over.

This slogan encourages you to check in with yourself at the end of the day too. Perhaps you could review your day in a journal before going to bed, with the focus on whether you stuck to your intention to write. Don't beat yourself up if you didn't write, just look at what happened honestly, and make a fresh commitment to try again tomorrow.

Exercises

Commit to writing every day, even if it's only for ten minutes.

Write your own commitment prayer or statement. Perhaps you could type it up on a piece of card and get it laminated, or stick it on a Post-it where you write.

Try morning pages for a month to see if it works for you. You can write in notebook or on loose-leaf pages, but aim to fill three pages every day.

Begin a journal to review your writing practice at the end of each day. You don't have to write a lot, just acknowledge what works for you and what doesn't.

Slogan 42: Be patient either way

This slogan is about being patient no matter what happens in your life. The original slogan is: "*Whichever of the two occurs, be patient*," so whether things go well or badly, accept them as they are and be patient.

Life is unpredictable. Sometimes it seems as if you can do no wrong and you coast along on a wave of goodwill. At other times, not so much. You may struggle to get your life back on track, but things refuse to go your way. This slogan tells you to be patient either way – during the good times and the bad times.

When things go wrong it isn't because you've made a mistake – it's just life changing. Everything changes so your circumstances will change too. You have limited control over the reality outside your head, so the only thing you can do is be patient.

When you see that you can't control everything, it makes you more humble. You begin to see how much it hurts both you and others to hold on to things you can't control, and slowly you learn to let go. You allow things to be as they are and let life unfold in its own way and in its own time. No grasping at the things you desire or running away from the things you fear.

Being patient means staying centred and focused on your intention to be free and awake. You can only do that in the present moment. So what this slogan is really saying is that you need to practice mind training and meditation all the time, no matter what is happening in your life.

When life is going well, you feel happy and in control, so you might think you don't need to meditate. You're happy enough, and besides, you're far too busy enjoying yourself. But when things go wrong and life gets crazy, you're too busy dealing with all your problems to sit for half an hour and breathe. Maybe you think you don't have time to meditate, or you're too upset or too stressed.

But this is exactly why you need to practice. And when better to get into a routine and develop your mindfulness muscles than when life is relatively calm. If you practice when life is good, you will have a solid grounding in mindfulness to draw upon when life goes bad. Plus you will be able to deal with whatever life throws at you more effectively because you will be coming from a place of calm focus instead.

So this slogan tells you not to wait for the perfect moment to meditate. Don't wait for events in your life to calm down and become controllable before you begin to take charge of your own mind.

To practice patience, simply be present with whatever is happening. Accept things as they come and go. Let go and let it be.

For Writers

The mutability of life can make it difficult to settle into a routine. Surprise upsets and detours can hijack your best intentions and trip you up just when you think you have everything under control. There isn't really anything you can do about it – life will change and so will you. But none of this gives you an excuse to avoid writing.

This slogan encourages you to write no matter what else is going on in your life. Don't wait for the perfect conditions that will allow you to write for hours, days, or months, uninterrupted and distraction free. You can't use the excuse that your life is just too crazy for you to write. Life is always crazy, one way or another. You're going to have to write anyway.

Equally, when life is going well and you're happily writing every day, don't assume this idyllic situation will last forever. Plan for upsets and be organised. Don't take the circumstances of your life for granted. The best way to do this is to write regardless of what is happening. Good, bad, or indifferent, you must write.

However, the process of writing can't be forced. You can't rush ahead of yourself and get to the end before you've written the rest of the story – even if you know how it ends. You need to trust the process and allow the writing to unfold in its own time.

This is easy when the writing is going well. When your writing isn't working as you hoped, be patient with yourself. Sometimes you're simply having a bad day and tomorrow will be better – or at least different. You can be certain the situation will change because it always does. The only way to improve bad writing is to keep writing and keep learning. So keep going, trust the process, trust yourself, and don't stop writing.

When you're having a good day, don't get caught up in fantasies about how brilliant you are and how many people are going to adore your work. The good writing days are great, and we all wish they would happen more often, but don't expect it to continue. Let the writing pour forth and make the most of it, but it won't always be that easy. Just enjoy it while it lasts, and keep writing.

The same patience is needed when you're picking your way through the jungle of success and failure in the world of publishing. Whether you're trying to get a book deal, or sell a story or an article, there are a lot of factors you can't control. Even once your book, story, or article is published, you can't control whether anyone will read it, never mind enjoy it.

Success requires patience because you will be expected to repeat your performance and produce more writing that will generate more success, and so on. It's a wonderful problem to have, but trying to hold on to success out of fear of losing it, will only damage your ability to write something well enough for it to succeed.

Failure requires patience for obvious reasons. It can take a long time to achieve the success you crave, and there is a lot of work and waiting involved in the meantime. The future always feels just out of reach while you write and wait and wait and write. You're waiting for your work to come to fruition, waiting for your big break, waiting for the right person to read your work and recognise your untapped genius.

When life isn't tripping you up with unexpected changes, it's making you wait for what you want – for the rain to stop, for the computer to boot up, for your phone to charge, for the kettle to boil, for someone to get back to you about that thing you've forgotten because you've been waiting so long...

Whether you succeed or fail in the writing business, you have to learn patience. Your writing may be good or bad, it may succeed or fail, but you can't hold on to either because it will soon change. So this slogan reminds you to accept both sides of life and to allow things to be just as they are.

Exercises

Make a cup of tea. Go ahead! But don't rush. Be patient while you wait for the kettle to boil and for the tea to brew. Practice being present for every step of the process. Don't get annoyed if you spill the milk – be patient!

Drink your tea! But don't rush. Savour every mouthful and really taste the tea. Let the moment be what it is.

In your slogan journal, write about your experience making and drinking tea while practising patience. What did you learn?

Slogan 43: Remember what's at stake

This slogan is about walking your talk and remembering to focus on what matters to you most – your intention to wake up and help others.

The original slogan is: *"Observe these two, even at the risk of your life,"* the two being the refuge and bodhisattva vows mentioned in Slogan 23. Don't be intimidated by the idea of taking these vows. It just means that you're making a commitment to free yourself so you can be happier and help others to do the same.

The refuge vow involves placing your faith in the Buddha, the teachings, and the spiritual community. It is a commitment to awaken to your true Self as Buddha nature, to grow in knowledge and understanding, and to support your fellow travellers on the path. The bodhisattva vow means doing this for the benefit of all sentient beings. In other words, it's about honouring life and living with compassion and wisdom.

These are noble aims and difficult to live up to, even on a good day. The original slogan says you should keep your vows even at the risk of your life – so this is serious stuff. It's about not wasting the opportunity you have in this precious life to wake up. It challenges you to do your best to live in a way that is beneficial and hopefully leaves the world a better place when you're gone.

What's at stake? Your happiness, perhaps, but what we're really talking about here is your soul. This is about your ability to live with yourself, to be able to look yourself in the eye and live up to your values and create a life worth living, a life filled with meaning and love and joy.

To live such a life is a real blessing and not everyone is so lucky. So if you have joy and love to spare, why wouldn't you share it?

What about those times when life is tough and you don't feel particularly enlightened, never mind happy? This slogan reminds you to keep practising and to do your best in every moment. Sometimes that's all you can do – your best. Try to stay awake and focused on your intention to be free. Be honest about your feelings and stay committed to helping others when you can. Even when it's hard, especially when it's hard, because that's when you and others need it the most.

This slogan reminds you that you don't make the vows or commitment once and then forget about it. Life is messy and complicated and you will be tempted to drift back to sleep, so you have to continually renew your vows. Every day, you need to remember what's at stake and why you are here.

The teachings aren't something you just read and think about. You actually have to put them into practice. Every single day. Don't go back to sleep! Stay focused because your life is at stake. Your life is on the line, but you're closer to freedom than you think. If who you really are is Buddha nature, then what is there to risk?

You're already free – you just have to remember how.

For Writers

This slogan reminds you how important writing is, especially when other parts of your life pull you away from your dreams. When you remember what's at stake, you write as if your life depends on it. That might seem an extreme way of looking at it, but any writer who doesn't write for any length of time, for whatever reason, would tell you that not writing when you need to write is a kind of personal hell.

The worst part of feeling blocked as a writer is that you want to write, but you don't know what to say, or how to say it. Or perhaps you don't know why you're writing anymore – it used to make sense, but now it feels hollow. So you stop writing.

This slogan asks you to think about what really matters to you. Imagine you're on your deathbed. Do you want to have regrets? Will you be saying, "*I wish I'd written a novel,*" "*I had a great idea for a story but never got around to writing it,*" or, "*I could have been a great poet if I'd followed my inspiration.*"

Don't keep putting it off. You don't know what's going to happen in your life, so take advantage of the time you have. You either want to write, or you don't. Use this slogan to remind you to stay committed to your writing goals. When you catch yourself making excuses because you haven't written anything today, be honest with yourself. What will happen if you keep making excuses?

Writing as if your life depends on it might give you a greater sense of urgency, like there's no time to waste, and you might get more done and feel more motivated. But it also might increase the pressure too much. This isn't about forcing yourself to write, or driving yourself to achieve the impossible. It's just about making the most of your talent and the opportunity you have to express yourself.

Don't waste your time doing things that don't really matter in the long run. But don't cling too fiercely to your dreams either. If you want to write, you need be present and remember to savour the moment. Now is the only time you can be fully present and alive, and that is also the best way to write – from the centre, the heart of your life.

It's also worth remembering that there are many people around the world who risk their lives to write in countries where freedom of speech is curtailed. When you feel your commitment slipping and you begin to wonder why you bother to write at all, think about what you would do in this situation. How deep is your commitment to your writing?

Would you write even at the risk of your life?

Exercises

In your slogan journal, explore the meaning of your life. Why are you alive? What do you live for? Why are you here?

Do some research: find out about writers who have lost their lives or have been imprisoned because of their work.

In your slogan journal, explore your feelings about the writers you learned about in your research. Were you inspired? Intimidated? Could you do what they did?

Slogan 44: Train in the three difficulties

This slogan is about how you deal with your bad habits and difficult emotions. The original slogan is the same and refers to the three difficulties of breaking free of your habitual patterns of behaviour. First you notice the habit, then you break the habit, and finally you resolve to keep practising until the habit is dissolved. Easy!

You might believe that the big problems in your life are the ones that cause the most difficulty, but actually it's the small ways you undermine yourself, moment by moment, that cause the most damage. These are your emotional and mental habits, the way you tend to react without thinking.

The three difficulties are the three ways your habits can cause problems. **First is the difficulty of seeing your habits**. If you want to change your mental and emotional habits, you have to notice what they are and catch them in action. But this isn't easy because they're hidden and you don't notice what you're doing until it's too late.

These habits are often emotional reactions that are rooted in the early patterns you learned as a child. They're hard to break because thinking about them doesn't seem to help much, and this is why they can be hard to spot. Something happens to trigger a reaction and the emotion comes up and takes over before you get a say in the matter.

So the first step is to really pay attention to what you're doing and feeling and thinking. See if you can spot any patterns. What keeps coming up? Do you always react the same way in certain situations? Watch your automatic responses and notice what happens. Don't judge – just notice.

The second difficulty is to break your habits once you've noticed them. Habits can be stubborn. No matter how hard you try to stop doing something, you keep doing it anyway. You need to interrupt the cycle of reaction, perhaps by doing something else. Shift your focus and replace the bad habit with a good habit.

You might like to analyse your habits to understand why you react the way you do. But be careful of this because it can become an endless cycle of questioning and self-examination going round and round inside your head. The real problem is often an ego attachment or defence mechanism: deep down you're just trying to protect yourself or make yourself feel better because you're insecure. So if you can let go of the ego, the emotional reactivity should diminish of its own accord.

When you notice a bad habit, don't repress what you're feeling. This process isn't about denying your difficult emotions or scary thoughts. You need to be honest with yourself about what comes up because only then will you be able to let it go and move on. So notice what happens and perhaps stop and take a deep breath. Don't beat yourself up for reacting the way you have, just stop and let it go.

The third difficulty is that once you have let your bad habit go, it tends to come back. You keep reacting the same way again and again, even though you know you don't want to. The only way to deal with this is to keep practising, keep letting it go. Remind yourself that you want to be free of this bad habit and keep doing your best.

The key to this slogan is you have to get sick of your bad habits before you're willing to change them. You have to *want* to change, and then you will.

For Writers

This slogan is about paying attention to all the ways you undermine yourself and stop yourself from writing. Your bad habits and neurotic tendencies may be small or large, but if you keep allowing them to control your choices you will never achieve your writing goals.

So the first step is to identify exactly what you are doing and how you are leading yourself astray. Notice which of your habits stop you from writing and find ways to overcome them. This isn't easy and you can't do it by simply deciding to do so. Every day you will have to confront and challenge yourself to not give in to your bad habits.

You may catch yourself getting into the habit of not writing because it's easier than writing. Before beginning any challenging task, there's always a period of inertia and resistance. You know you have work to do but balk at the thought of it. Sometimes you would do almost anything rather than write. But if you allow this procrastination to continue, it could become a habit.

When you give in to the inertia and begin to actively avoid writing, you're giving yourself a powerful message. You're saying that writing doesn't matter that much to you. Then the next time you sit down to write, you will start to feel negatively inclined towards your work. It may start as simple avoidance, but over time it can turn into an active hatred. And that can spiral out of control into self-doubt and worse.

Inertia and resistance are natural parts of the creative process so you won't be able to get rid of them completely. But you can break the habit of avoidance and resolve to write even when it's hard and scary.

If you want to write, you need to create a habit of writing. And the best way to do that is to write every day, regardless how you feel about it. Just write something. Anything. Even if you write about how you don't want to write anything, you will be giving yourself a positive message through your actions.

You can take control of your mind and stop it from being hijacked by your doubts and fears. These are what drive your habits and stop you from writing. So this slogan encourages you to notice what stops you from writing and to break those habits and let them go. Beyond that, there is only one thing you need to do:

Keep writing.

Exercises

In your slogan journal, list all your bad habits. Be honest with yourself – nobody else has to see your list.

Which of these habits stop you from writing? What is at the root of your avoidance? What can you do to change your behaviour?

Think of at least ten positive ways you can support your writing.

If you haven't written anything today, do it now. Go ahead – put this down and write something.

Slogan 45: Take on the three causes

This slogan is about increasing the possibility of awakening by embracing ideas and practices that support you. The original slogan is: "*Take on the three principal causes*," which means doing the three things that will cause you to awaken.

The three causes are: finding a teacher, embracing the teachings, and developing a lifestyle that supports your desire to awaken. Taking on these causes will help you to overcome the bad habits we looked at in Slogan 44 because they support your desire to change and be free of negativity.

Before you can even begin to practice, you need to be aware that you have a choice in the first place – that it is possible to be free and awake and happy. You won't practice meditation and learn how to awaken if you don't know that you can. So **the first cause is finding a teacher**.

A teacher could be an individual or a community of like-minded friends, somebody who inspires you to embark on the spiritual path and start practising. It doesn't have to be a recognised spiritual teacher; it could be one of your friends, a book or an article online, or just something you stumble across that piques your interest.

The initial encounter with the teacher can also come from within. Perhaps you have a peak experience or a sudden shift in your consciousness that opens up your mind to wider possibilities. Or you gain an unexpected insight into your behaviour that makes you want to find out more and dig deeper. Whatever it is, the teacher inspires you to want to wake up.

The second cause is recognising the importance of the teachings and the need to train your mind. Once you have been inspired you have to put the teachings into practice and follow through with your intention to wake up. Meditation and mind training are practical – you can't just read about them or listen to a teacher. You have to practice.

Inspiration may get you moving to begin with, but you have to keep going through all life's ups and downs. You have to confront your bad habits and make changes that are hard to maintain, and practice even when you don't feel inspired. The teachings will support you along the path and remind you that you're not alone. Others have walked this path before you and have overcome the very problems you are struggling with now.

The third cause is to change your lifestyle so it supports your desire to practice and awaken. This is especially true when you are struggling because it's easy to let your problems get in the way of your practice, when really your practice should be helping with your problems.

This means that you need to ensure you have enough stability in your life so you can dedicate time and energy to meditation and any other practices that you want to do. It's hard to focus on waking up when every day is a struggle just to get by.

So if you are lucky enough to have found a teacher and the inspiration to practice, and you have access to the teachings, you need to do your best to make the most of them. Don't waste the opportunity to awaken. You never know when you'll get the chance again.

For Writers

This slogan is about improving your chances of success by embracing ideas and practices that support your writing. When you get sidetracked and distracted by your busy life and begin to lose focus, taking on the three causes will help you to get back on track. When you feel like you're not getting anywhere or when you experience a setback in your work, this slogan can remind you to keep writing.

The three causes for writers are: find good teachers, learn and practice your craft, and organise your life so you can write.

The first cause is to find good teachers. Writing well is as much about inspiration as it is about craft. If you want to be a writer, you must be a voracious reader. Nobody reads as many books as writers. When you read a well-crafted story it triggers ideas you can't wait to explore and inspires you to try harder in your own work. Even bad books can provide inspiration because they show you what not to do.

But inspiration doesn't just come from reading. Writing groups can be a useful source of support, encouragement, and inspiration. Attending writing conferences or workshops where you can meet fellow writers and find supportive friends may also inspire you.

Once you have found good teachers, you need to embrace the second cause and put all this inspiration into practice. The most important thing you can do as a writer is practice. **You must learn and practice your craft**. Good writers do a lot of writing. Not just writing, but rewriting. And editing and revising and complete demolition and rebuilding. And then more writing. And rewriting. And... you get the idea.

Learning your craft comes from practising your craft, by writing. But you will also need to get feedback on your work. If you have found good teachers, they can help with this, and you can also share your work and get notes from your writing group and supportive friends. There are also online support groups that you can join.

Writers are generally a helpful bunch and tend to share their knowledge and experience. There is a wealth of helpful advice online, but it's worth exercising some discrimination. It's no good getting feedback or advice from people who don't know what they're doing or who don't understand you and what you're trying to achieve. The best feedback and editorial support will come from individuals who are professional enough to keep their personal feelings out of the advice they offer.

All this inspiration and support and advice will be of no use to you if you don't embrace the third cause. **You must organise your life so you can write**. This can be a challenge, but it's not impossible, and if you really want to write you will find the time – or make the time – to write. If your lifestyle doesn't support your need to write on a regular basis, you will need to make some changes.

Whatever else you do, the most important thing is to focus on the writing. Make the changes you need to make and concentrate on becoming a better writer, because in the end, that's the only thing you can control.

Exercises

Who are your teachers? Make a list in your slogan journal.

What inspired you to become a writer? Write about the experience in your slogan journal.

Look at how your life is organised. Do you have enough time to write? If not, what can you change?

Slogan 46: Don't lose track

This slogan is about using gratitude to maintain your commitment to the three causes in Slogan 45. The original slogan is: *"Pay heed that the three never wane,"* which means remembering the inspiration of your teacher, practising the teachings, and the importance of a supportive lifestyle.

It's hard to maintain your enthusiasm and keep practising over the many years it can take to wake up – and it could take a lifetime. You feel inspired at the start of your practice, but can soon lose track of what you're trying to do. So this slogan encourages you to practice gratitude and discipline in relation to the three causes of the last slogan.

First you need to be grateful to your teachers and community and for the fact that you found the inspiration to begin practising. You were only able to discover the possibility of becoming free and waking up to your true Self because of teachers who dedicate their lives to passing on the teachings. Don't take your teachers for granted – they are a precious gift.

Next is gratitude for the teachings themselves. You are lucky to have found a teaching that helps you to become happier. Imagine what would have happened to you if you hadn't discovered a way to overcome your suffering and wake up to your true nature. The best way to express your gratitude for the teachings is to practice them consistently and to share what you learn with others. Pay it forward – pass on the benefit to others.

Finally, you need the discipline to keep practising and ensure that your lifestyle enables you to do so. Discipline sounds boring and like hard work, but it's really just a case of developing positive, life-affirming habits instead of letting things slide and falling back into bad habits.

Through the ups and downs of life, your practice can become the one thing you know you can rely on. Your true Self is always there, underneath the confusion and distraction and craziness. Buddha nature is the one thing that will never let you down – surely that's something worth being grateful for.

The point of this slogan is to keep you on track. When you feel yourself slipping it reminds you to be grateful and to step up your practice. Practising gratitude means you're much less likely to take things for granted and you won't waste the opportunity to wake up and remember who you really are.

For Writers

This slogan encourages you to stay focused on the three causes of the previous slogan: finding good teachers, learning and practising your craft, and organising your life so you can write. Don't lose track of your inspiration and reasons for writing.

Your initial inspiration to become a writer probably came from reading other writers, and your greatest teachers will be the writers who came before you. They will have struggled to write, exactly as you do now. But they also found a way to overcome their doubts and write anyway – so you can too. Be grateful for the inspiration to write, no matter where it comes from, and remember to honour your teachers.

This slogan also encourages you to be grateful for the opportunity to learn and practice your craft. It can take a long time to master the skills you need in order to express yourself the way you dream of doing, and in the meantime it's easy to get distracted or discouraged. You can't learn without the support and feedback from other writers, whether in person or via the internet and craft books. There has never been such a wealth of information available to anyone, anywhere, so be grateful for your writing friends.

Finally, this slogan encourages you to keep writing. No matter what else is going on in your life, if you want to write you have to find the discipline to keep writing. This is a lot easier if your life is organised in a way that supports your desire to write. So if you haven't written for a while, this slogan can remind you to get back on track.

Practising gratitude for the people and circumstances that support you will help you to keep writing, and encourage you to refresh your inspiration on a regular basis. Remember that there is a reason you wanted to write. Don't let your inspiration whither away through lack of appreciation.

The best way to maintain your focus and the discipline to keep writing when life gets difficult is to remember to be grateful for the opportunity to write at all. You never know, you might end up writing something that inspires another person to become a writer.

Exercises

Look at your list of teachers from the previous slogan. Choose your top three inspirations and write in your slogan journal about how and why these individuals are so important to you.

What are your reasons for writing? Make a list in your slogan journal.

Choose your top three reasons for writing and explore them in more depth. What are your reasons for having these reasons? What desires or needs are you hoping to fulfil through your writing?

Imagine you have become an inspiration to other writers. Write about why you think they find your writing inspirational. This will give you clues as to the kind of writing you should be doing.

Slogan 47: Practice with your whole being

This slogan is about applying the practice of mind training to your whole being, not just your mind. The original slogan is: *"Keep the three inseparable,"* which means seeing the body, speech, and mind as united.

Mind training isn't just about what goes on inside your head. It may appear that the focus is on learning to master your thoughts, but this slogan makes it clear that the mind needs to work with the body and speech. The body refers to how you act and what you do. Speech refers to your emotions and is the whole range of how you express yourself, not just what you say. Finally, mind is the obvious part – how you think.

When you practice meditation it doesn't just affect your thinking. It also feeds into every other part of your life. When you feel calm and focused, your actions tend to come from a more considered place. Perhaps you rush less because you feel more relaxed. You might sleep better because you feel less stressed and this will boost your energy levels. And you're more likely to take care of yourself physically because you can see where your bad habits are causing suffering.

On an emotional level you may feel less anxious and reactive, so it's easier to express yourself in a compassionate and friendly way. Perhaps you feel less self-centred and more open, and this improves your relationships with others.

Your thinking also calms down and becomes less compulsive. You're less likely to get caught up in obsessive thoughts and worries over things you can't control. There may be more space in your head, more room for your mind to stretch out and explore, and your thinking becomes clearer and more focused.

When this calm mind is combined with less stressful emotions you're more likely to express yourself positively. Your speech becomes more compassionate, and maybe you will listen more carefully, rather than jumping in to share your opinions without thinking.

When you practice with your whole being it means you act, speak and think with compassion and wisdom. This slogan reminds you to apply your mind training practice to your whole life and not just to what goes on inside your head. Mind training and meditation are also about what you do when you get off the meditation cushion and interact with the rest of the world.

And it all starts with the way you think. As you think, so you become.

For Writers

Writing is another activity that's often seen as being just about the mind and thinking. There is a lot of thinking involved, but there's more to it than that. Writing well comes from your whole being, not just your mind. Your whole life influences what comes out when you sit down to write.

> "Writing is a practice of looking deeply... Even before we begin writing, during whatever we are doing – gardening or sweeping the floor – our book or essay is being written deep down in our consciousness. To write a book we must write with our whole life, not just during the moments we are sitting at our desk." – Thich Nhat Hanh

How you think affects the way you act and talk and write. When your mind is unfocused your thinking will be undisciplined and sloppy, and then you can't expect your writing to be clear either. Practising meditation and mind training will help to focus your mind because it brings you back in touch with your body.

One of the quickest ways to clear your head is to stop what you're doing and take a series of deep breaths. This calms your nervous system and creates an open space in your mind. The clamour of your thoughts will die away as you come back to yourself, present in this moment.

The body is always present in the now, it has no concept of time. It's your mind that creates the feeling of time passing, always rushing ahead into the future. This causes your thoughts to race to keep up and you start to feel stressed and scattered. You can't write when you feel like this.

When you're out of touch with your body, you will also be out of touch with your feelings and the deeper needs of your soul because they communicate through the body more than the mind. When you're grounded in your body through the breath, your thinking is clearer and more focused.

So this slogan encourages you to write with your whole being. Before you begin to write, take a moment to focus on your body by taking deep calming breaths. From this rooted place you will be able to hear the still small voice of your intuition more clearly and tap into the guidance of your true Self. You may find that your writing flows more easily when you do this because it brings you into the present moment.

Another way to apply this slogan is to remember to use all the senses in your writing. Your descriptions and prose feel more real when you show not just what a character is seeing and thinking, but what they can hear, taste, smell, and touch too. Staying grounded in your own body will also help you to feel what your characters are feeling, and this makes for more vivid writing.

Writing with your whole being is also about the desire to communicate from the heart and really connect with others. What you feel and experience can be channelled into your writing, and to do this most effectively means you must stay in touch with what you are feeling.

If you write from the head, without grounding your words in a lived experience, the reader will feel the disconnect and the words just won't land. Your writing won't feel real because you haven't allowed it to take form and come to life. When you are present in your writing, then the reader will be more likely to feel it too.

This slogan reminds you that writing is an action that you do with your whole being. As you write, so you are. As you are, so you write.

Exercises

Get your slogan journal and a pen but don't write anything – yet. Spend five minutes taking deep calming breaths. Close your eyes if you like. Don't think. When you're ready, pick up the pen and write. Again, don't think – just write and see what happens.

In your slogan journal, write for five minutes about where you're sitting. Include all the senses: what can you see, hear, smell, taste, and touch?

Try to capture one of your most vivid memories in words. Write about what happened using all the senses and really bring the moment to life, as if you are reliving the experience.

Slogan 48: Train with a whole heart

This slogan is about applying the practice of mind training to everything in your life, not just when you're meditating. It continues from the previous slogan where you practice with your whole being and asks you to extend that to the rest of your life.

The original slogan is rather long: *"Train without bias in all areas. It is crucial always to do this pervasively and wholeheartedly."* The key idea is to practice without bias, which means you practice with everything that happens. Include everyone and all experiences, with no exceptions.

Training with a whole heart means you don't discriminate – you approach everything in the same way, with openness and compassion. It means your whole life is an experiment in how present you can be, and how willing you are to really face whatever is happening at any given moment.

This slogan is telling you not to split your life into meditation on the one hand, and then everything else on the other. Mind training isn't just about what happens while you are sitting on your meditation cushion. It also applies to how you deal with other people and the ups and downs of life.

You may be able to meditate your way into a calm and relaxed state of mind, but if you lose the plot as soon as a challenging situation arises, then you're not really practising – you're running away. Meditation isn't about avoidance; it's about confronting life head on and dealing with whatever comes up with an open mind and heart.

So practice isn't just meditation, practice is also life. Real life is where your meditation practice will be tested to see how well you are learning to let go of your own agenda and open yourself to compassion. If there's something in your life that is particularly painful or difficult, you won't be able to avoid it in meditation. In fact, this is exactly the stuff you need to be working with.

Anything can be used to train your mind, any experience or feeling, good or bad, easy or difficult. Don't compartmentalise your life or avoid the darker side of your experience, because it's the difficult stuff that often helps you to grow more. You tend to learn more when bad things happen because you're more likely to dig deeper into your experience in search of answers.

So this slogan challenges you to accept every part of your life and every part of yourself. Nothing is off-limits. Be indiscriminate with your compassion. Be totally democratic and even-handed in your approach. Don't hide from yourself or avoid people you don't like or circumstances that you find difficult. When you train with a whole heart, everything can help you to cultivate compassion and wisdom.

For Writers

This slogan encourages you to write with a whole heart, which follows from the previous slogan about writing with your whole being. They seem similar and there is some overlap, but here the emphasis is on embracing the whole of your experience, inside and out.

Everything in your life can be used in your writing: all of your feelings, thoughts, and experiences, both good and bad. But if there are aspects of yourself that make you feel uncomfortable or parts of your experience that you tend to avoid, you may find it difficult to create fully rounded characters for your stories. To be believable, characters need to be multidimensional. They need to have access to the full range of emotions and experience that make stories compelling. So you need to be willing to explore those feelings yourself.

Obviously this doesn't mean that if you want to write a story about a murderer that you have to go out and kill someone! That would be taking research a little too far. But in your imagination you would have to be willing to follow the character into some pretty dark places.

Writing with a whole heart means including the whole of life in your writing – the joy and the sorrow and everything in between. This slogan encourages you to exclude nothing from your experience. You can open yourself to everything and allow it to speak through you. Writing with a whole heart, without bias, can bring forth stories from characters whose voices might never be heard otherwise.

Another way to apply this slogan is to look at any biases you have towards your writing. Perhaps you are happy with your description and prose but struggle with dialogue. Maybe your storylines are brilliantly realised but your characters feel flat. Or perhaps you enjoy writing short stories and long to write a novel, but every time you try the story unravels halfway through.

This slogan encourages you to embrace all of your writing – not just the parts you like and enjoy, but even the parts you don't like. Embrace everything: your mistakes, false starts, bad writing, clumsy characterisation, embarrassing dialogue, and half-finished stories. There is nothing wrong with any of this stuff. You might not want anybody else to read it, but you learn from it all.

There is only one way to become a better writer and that is to write badly and to learn from your mistakes and try again. In the process, you also learn something about yourself. You learn that you can open yourself to any experience, no matter how difficult or painful, and you can take it into yourself and transform it into something meaningful.

Exercises

Look at the characters that feature in your stories. Do you always write a certain type? Are there any character types you tend to avoid? In your slogan journal, explore your characters and see what you can learn about yourself.

Are there any subject areas or emotional experiences that you avoid in your writing? If so, why?

Find a story or poem that you abandoned as a lost cause. Read it with a whole heart – without bias – and notice how it feels. Write about your reaction and what you can learn from it.

We often write what we need to learn. What are your stories trying to teach you?

Slogan 49: Meditate on what you resent

This slogan is about noticing when you shut down or get annoyed and using that to wake yourself up. The original slogan is: *"Always meditate on whatever provokes resentment,"* and it encourages you to practice tonglen meditation with the things that get your goat.

Life often fails to live up to your expectations. When things don't go the way you want, you feel resentment. So this slogan challenges you to work directly with all these little annoyances – the situations and people who make you angry or upset, as well as parts of yourself that you don't like.

When you notice yourself reacting negatively and feeling resentful, turn it into a meditation practice. The idea is to transform your resentment into acceptance. On a simple level, you can just take a few deep breaths and let the negativity go. But if you want to go deeper, you can practice tonglen with it. Breathe in the resentment, the irritation, or the anger, and breathe out acceptance.

This slogan asks you to pay attention to the things that disturb your peace of mind and work with them rather than pushing them away. Every time you react automatically and get annoyed because something hasn't gone the way you hoped, you're giving in to the smaller, petty side of yourself – the ego.

The ego reacts with anger and resentment as a defence against reality. But shouting about the injustice of life and how you have been hurt is just a way to avoid feeling what you are really feeling. Underneath the anger there's usually a sore spot, something you don't want to face. Reacting with anger may feel safer than acknowledging you feel scared or powerless or humiliated.

When something doesn't go your way it makes you feel small and reminds you that you're not really in control – you're not the centre of the universe. But rather than let that truth sink in and learn to move beyond the ego to the true Self, you put up defences and get angry and resentful. You push back against reality.

It can be disheartening when you see how much of your thinking is pushing against reality. It's as if you are constantly saying no – no, I don't like that, don't want that, it's not right, it's not good enough, and so on. When you do this, you're trying to control life and fighting against yourself.

This slogan provides a way to turn resistance into liberation by noticing when you react and going straight to the heart of the feeling rather than turning away. Instead of fighting against reality you can learn to open up and accept things as they are.

Resentment is resistance of reality – but resistance is futile! When you stop resisting reality the truth is revealed. You embrace your true nature and see that you are the universe. There is no need to fight reality or feel scared and powerless.

For Writers

Writing can be a frustrating process even when it's going well. Inspiration strikes and you rush to write it down, but the end result often falls short of your imagination. So you work hard to perfect your idea, crafting and rewriting, slowly transforming it into something you're happy to share. But when you show your work you don't get the reaction you were hoping for – it gets rejected, or harshly criticised, or simply ignored.

It's natural to feel resentment when this happens. You've put in so much work and effort and time, the very least somebody could do is acknowledge what you have achieved. But your readers don't owe you anything. It's not their job to fulfil your expectations. You can't control how people will respond to your work, but you can control how you respond to their responses.

This slogan encourages you to meditate on your resentment instead of brooding on it and feeling sorry for yourself. When your work is rejected you can turn it into an opportunity to learn something about your expectations and the dreams you secretly hope to fulfil.

For example, because you've been meditating faithfully for years, you may believe that you're not too bothered by other people's reactions to your writing. It's great when they enjoy your work, but if they don't, it's no big deal. That is until you try to sell your magnum opus – a novel you've been working on, secretly, for years. And nobody wants it.

When this happens and you find yourself eaten alive by resentment and anger, it's a sign that your ego is still firmly attached to your writing and that you have a lot more work to do in your meditation practice. And possibly with your book too.

These kinds of negative reactions can take you by surprise, but if you watch yourself through an average day, you will probably notice yourself reacting with irritation more often than you would care to admit.

You go to print out a story and the paper jams in the printer. You're just sitting down to write and the phone rings. You come up with a brilliant idea while you're doing the weekly shop and what with one thing and another by the time you manage to find a piece of paper to scribble it down, you've forgotten it. You've been struggling with your writing for years and your best friend suddenly decides to write a poem – never written one before – and wins a competition. Grrr!

Use this slogan to practice with little things that irritate you through the day, and then when something major happens – like your book gets rejected, again! – you may be able to accept it more easily.

It's important to note that this process of turning resentment into acceptance isn't about giving up. You don't abandon your dreams or the goals you're trying to achieve just because you meet a little resistance. You can learn a lot about yourself by observing how you react to disappointments and setbacks. Meditating on your resentment can reveal where you feel stuck and scared, and that can help you to zone in on what needs more work.

In the end, this slogan is about alchemy – taking a negative reaction and turning it into understanding and wisdom.

Exercises

In your slogan journal, list the things that get your goat. Don't do this for too long – irritants have a tendency to breed and multiply – stop when you have filled a page.

Decide on your top five irritants – the things that fill you with the most resentment – and explore the feelings behind them. What can you learn about yourself from your negative reactions?

What are your expectations in relation to your writing? What do you hope to achieve? How do you hope others will react to your work? Write in your journal.

As a thought experiment, imagine that you will never fulfil your writing expectations. Go through each doomed expectation and explore your feelings about its impending failure. What will you do if never finish your novel? What will you do if you never achieve publication? What will you do if you're never hailed as a genius?! What will you do if you're never respected, listened to, read, widely shared, talked about, successful, rich...?

Slogan 50: Don't count on external conditions

This slogan is about practising mind training no matter what is going on in your life. Whether your circumstances are favourable or not, practice anyway.

The original slogan is: *"Don't be swayed by external circumstances,"* which reminds you that you can't control reality. You can only control your reaction to it and you do this by practising regardless.

Life is unpredictable. Things are always changing and you can't predict the future. You never know what is going to happen next. Even when you plan carefully and try really hard to stay focused on your goals, life can still take you by surprise. This slogan reminds you that you can't count on things staying the same as they are now. When life is going well, don't count on it staying that way. This isn't what you want to hear, but when things aren't going well, it might be a relief to remember that it will soon change.

The point is that you can't use the fact of changing circumstances as an excuse to avoid mind training. You can't wait for the perfect moment to begin meditating because it will never arrive. You have to make do with the circumstances that you have, and that's going to be messy. And complicated and frustrating and sometimes surprisingly easy.

You may not be able to control external conditions but you can do something about your own thoughts. You can choose to meditate no matter what is happening or how you are feeling. The goal of mind training isn't to stop things from changing or to control how things turn out or even to know what to do. You practice mind training so you can deal with whatever happens in a more flexible and patient way.

Meditation means turning your mind towards your experience, towards the reality of your life. As we saw with the previous slogan, it's not an excuse to avoid things you don't like, but an invitation to open up and accept things as they are. When you meditate, you work with whatever comes up. For example, with tonglen meditation, when your life is going well, you can breathe out your happiness for others to enjoy, and when life isn't so good, you can breathe in your suffering and dissolve it in compassion.

Meditation and mindfulness can be practised all the time – you don't have to sit and focus on your breath if circumstances make that difficult. You can still choose to pay attention to whatever is happening with mindfulness and a willingness to be present. You don't have to wait for your life to be perfect before you start to practice, and there is no need to use difficult circumstances as an excuse to avoid it. You can practice anyway.

No matter what is going on, whether your external conditions are favourable or not, your true Self is always there and you can always come home to it. You may not be able to count on external conditions, but you can count on your Buddha nature.

For Writers

Writers are very inventive when it comes to making excuses to avoid writing. One of the worst excuses is that the circumstances of your life don't support your desire to write. You may convince yourself that you would love to write a novel, if only you had the time. Perhaps you'll get round to it later, when things are less hectic, when you can take some time off work, when you retire, when you win the lottery. The excuses are endless, and they don't always relate to the issue of time.

Perfect conditions come in many shapes and sizes. Perhaps you need peace and quiet with no distractions or interruptions, the right pen, a snazzy notebook, a better computer, your own office, a group of cheerleaders, an adoring entourage or fan club, five cups of coffee, perfect health, a genius idea, guaranteed success, better childcare facilities, a book deal, an agent, no day job, a magical supply of money, brandy, higher book sales, to be Neil Gaiman, an ergonomic chair, an enormous oak desk, a quill...

You get the idea. Whatever your excuses may be, this slogan reminds you not to count on external conditions. Life is too messy and unpredictable and you can't always make things work the way you want. If you wait for the perfect conditions in which to write, you will never write anything.

Look at the excuses you make when the conditions of your life aren't perfect and ask yourself if there's anything you can do about them. Some of the conditions you think you need may not be so necessary and you should be able to work around them. Others may be easy to fix. If you need more time, reorganise your schedule and delegate some of your responsibilities. If you need support, join a writing group.

If you need a quill – get over yourself!

Waiting for the perfect conditions can also apply to how you feel about your writing. Perhaps you want to write but don't know where to start. You feel confused and want to wait until you feel like you know what you're doing. Maybe every time you try to write something you think it's so terrible that you give up in shame.

But if you wait until you know what you're doing, you will never begin. And if you wait until you can write well enough, you will never improve. Writing is one of those things that you can only learn by actually doing it. That means you have to accept that much of what you write will be excruciating and embarrassing. But you will only improve through practice.

The more you write, the better you will get – perhaps. It's not a case of simply producing an enormous quantity of words. You have to learn from your mistakes too. So perhaps it should say: the more you rewrite, the better you will get.

The only thing of which you can be certain is that your circumstances will change. You can't always control external conditions but you can control your attitude, so whether you write or not is up to you.

Exercises

In your slogan journal, list all the excuses you have used to avoid writing.

Describe your ideal writing day. What perfect conditions do you believe you need in order to write?

Now is the perfect time to write something. Put this down and write – no excuses!

Slogan 51: Practice what's important

This slogan is about not wasting the opportunity to practice mind training by paying attention to this moment right now. The original slogan is: "*This time, practice the main points,*" which are to help others, practice the teachings, and cultivate compassion.

This moment is the only time in which you can live, so it's important to not waste your precious time and energy on things that don't really matter, especially if they don't make you happy or help you to wake up. Right now is the only time you can choose to change the way you live to become happier and more awake.

You can only practice meditation now. Whatever else is going on, now is the time to be disciplined and pay attention. Focus on what's happening now and drop the internal chatter. Breathe, let go, do whatever you need to do, but do it right now, because that is the only moment that exists.

The important point to remember is that mind training and meditation are about awakening to who you really are as Buddha nature. You may think you meditate because it helps you to feel calm, or it reduces stress or makes you healthier, but ultimately, it's not really about you. Even trying to awaken to your true nature isn't about you.

When you recognise your Buddha nature you see how everything is interdependent and constantly changing and intimately part of who you are on a fundamental level. If this is so, then it makes no sense to focus all your time and energy on yourself. All you're going to do is make yourself miserable in the long run because focusing on yourself cuts you off from the meaning and flow of life.

So this slogan encourages you to remember this truth and to put it into practice by being of service to others. Make yourself available to be whatever life needs you to be and help others as best you can. One of the ways you can do this is to observe the second point, which is to actually practice the teachings. Embody the teachings in your own life as best you can and share what you learn with others.

When you do this you live in a way that cultivates compassion and wisdom. By paying attention to this moment and opening to the possibility of being of service in some way, you become a force for good in your own life and in the lives of others. Doing your best to treat others (and yourself) with compassion will reduce suffering and spread joy.

It doesn't matter how much you have struggled up to this point. Every moment is a fresh opportunity to practice. You can only wake up now. You can only practice now. You can only do you best now.

So practice what's important – now.

For Writers

This slogan reminds you to practice what's important, and if you're a writer, that means writing. There are so many distractions and enticing possibilities pulling at your attention, that your precious writing time can be frittered away before you even realise what has happened. But if you allow yourself to be pulled away from your writing, you have nobody but yourself to blame.

You know writing matters to you. You know it's important. So write.

This slogan is a gentle reminder that you have no time to waste, so you'd better get on with it. However, there may be times when a friendly prod isn't enough. There could be many reasons why you're struggling to write, so rather than beating yourself up for not writing, have a look at your life and try to determine what's going on.

Practising what's important means paying attention, so watch yourself as you make the decision to not write. You might not realise you're even making a choice. Your life might be so busy and filled with other important tasks that you assume you're not writing because of circumstances beyond your control. But as the previous slogan shows, you're not at the mercy of circumstances. You can choose to live in a different way.

Use this slogan to bring your attention to the present moment and really pay attention to what you're doing. Perhaps there are changes you can make that will help you to practice what's important. Don't assume you're a lost cause. There is always another chance to make a different choice.

If you didn't write yesterday, that's okay. You can write today.

Each new sentence is a fresh opportunity to say what you need to say, to bring what is hidden up into the light and give it a voice. Don't waste time worrying about all the times you got it wrong or wrote a bad sentence or got rejected or gave up and sat in front of the TV feeling sorry for yourself.

Every moment is a fresh opportunity to practice. Even if you keep messing up and letting it slide, it doesn't matter. As soon as you notice what you're doing, just let it go and inhabit this moment right now.

This time, this moment, you can get it right. You can write.

Exercises

Have you written today? If not, write something. Now!

In your slogan journal, explore what is important to you. What are your main priorities in life? Is writing on your list?

What is important about your writing? Why is writing important to you?

Slogan 52: Don't misinterpret

This slogan is about not misinterpreting the teachings or applying them in ways that mean you don't really have to change. The original slogan is the same and focuses on six specific qualities that you should avoid misinterpreting: patience, yearning, excitement, compassion, priorities, and joy.

Spiritual practices of all kinds are powerful and seductive, they make you feel good and can improve your life in so many ways. But you can also fool yourself if you're not careful. Meditation is designed to transcend the ego, but it can also be used to avoid problems and subtly boost the ego instead.

This happens when you misinterpret the teachings and only apply them when it suits you. Perhaps you believe that because you are calm and compassionate that your practice is going well, but really you're avoiding a deeper confrontation with the darker parts of yourself and reality. Instead of dealing with a problem directly, you try to rise above it. You tell yourself you're transcending the situation, or not being attached, or letting go, but in reality you're running away.

The teachings are hard to live up to and there will be times when it feels easier to look the other way and pretend that everything is fine. You try to fix your life into one predictable shape – a calm, serene, spiritual shape. But sooner or later this will backfire because life can't be fixed in place. You can't use the teachings to control reality and avoid change, so one way or another, you will have to face and deal with whatever you're running from.

This slogan reminds you to keep it real and be honest with yourself about what you're doing. You can practice with everything in your life and there is no need to abuse the teachings to make yourself look good. When difficult emotions come up, don't push them away or deny that you're feeling them. It's not a sign that you're doing something wrong and you haven't failed in your practice. Just turn towards the feeling and include it in your meditation.

There are six main qualities that you might be tempted to misinterpret, but you could also include any positive virtue that is open to misuse. When you misinterpret these qualities they become problematic and don't work the way they should. Rather than embodying positive virtues in a way that benefits everyone, you use them to feed your own ego.

For example, you might be patient when things are going well, but when things get difficult you have a meltdown. Or you apply patience to your life in a way that leads to problems, such as letting things slide rather than dealing with them, or being patient when it suits you but not when it means having to let something go.

Yearning and excitement are misinterpreted when you use them in service of your worldly goals, for example you yearn for spiritual power and status rather than for wisdom and compassion. Or you get excited by worldly distractions, such as money or the latest drama on Netflix rather than the possibility of awakening or sharing your knowledge.

Compassion is misinterpreted when you only apply it to the people you like or to those you believe deserve your help. In a similar way to misusing patience, you can make life difficult for yourself when you practice compassion without also applying some common sense. For example, you allow others to abuse and walk all over you rather than setting clear boundaries and saying no when they overstep the mark. This is what's called 'idiot compassion,' because it does nobody any good in the long run.

When you misinterpret priorities you have no trouble finding the time to do all sorts of other activities, but never get around to meditating. Or you focus more of your energy on achieving worldly success and forget about working towards achieving inner peace and happiness.

Finally, when you misinterpret joy you feel happy when your enemies, or people you don't like, experience suffering, perhaps believing that they're getting what they deserve, rather than rejoicing when others do well or experience happiness.

When you wilfully misinterpret the teachings it means you're not really practising. It's easy to practice when you have no problems and life appears calm. But you can also slip into bad habits and become complacent, and even start to believe that you're better than others because you're not struggling and they are.

Don't assume that when things are going well for you that everything is fine and that your practice is faultless. This slogan reminds you to check that you're not misinterpreting the teachings or disappearing into a spiritual fantasy world. If you want to awaken to your true nature, you have to walk your talk. It has to be real or it is just more delusion.

For Writers

There are many unknowns in the process of writing. You don't know if you will be able to finish the story you're writing, and you don't know if it will make sense even if you do. You don't know whether anybody else will enjoy your story. You don't know if your book will be published, and you don't know if it will sell. Sometimes you don't even know if you can write at all.

Faced with all this uncertainty, it's tempting to start making assumptions. You look at your writing and your life, and you jump to conclusions. Perhaps you believe that since nobody is interested in reading your work, you should stop writing. Or maybe you should write something different, more commercial, or give it away free. It worked for other writers; maybe it will work for you too.

There are no easy answers to any of these problems. So when you don't know what to do, you might be tempted to misinterpret your situation, and your feelings, in an attempt to make things seem more manageable. When everything is up in the air, you want to nail it down and control it. Uncertainty can lead to some very bad choices because there are too many things you don't know, and what you do know may not be reliable either.

This slogan encourages you to be careful how you interpret what's going on and what you're feeling. Don't take the rejection of your work as a sign that you should give up writing. It may simply be that your story needs a little more work, or that you need to send it to different people.

If you're having trouble finding the time to write or other problems are interfering with your writing, it doesn't necessarily mean you should quit. Perhaps you need to reorganise your schedule or get some support. Maybe you need to take a break to deal with your other problems, and then you can return to your writing refreshed.

Equally, if you're experiencing a period of success, don't take this as a sign that you finally know what you're doing. When things are going well, it's not necessarily a sign that you can slack off and think you've arrived at the summit. If you misinterpret your success in this way you could become complacent and this may have a negative impact on the quality of your writing.

Another way to work with this slogan is to look at how you interpret the six qualities in relation to your writing. For example, perhaps you are being too patient waiting for your book to be picked up by a publisher. If you're still sending out your manuscript after a year of trying, perhaps you should consider alternatives, such as self-publishing.

Look at your attitudes and assumptions about success and ask yourself whether you are more focused on achieving world domination as an author than on forming a genuine connection with your readers. Perhaps you care more about book sales than the desire to improve your writing. Getting your priorities mixed up like this or feeling excitement over things you can't control won't help you become a better writer.

In writing, you're always at the beginning and you'll never reach a point where everything you do makes perfect sense. You will never really know what you're doing, and problems will always come up because that's the way life works. Life will surprise and upset you, but you don't have to let that stop you from writing.

Don't let the uncertainty of life interfere with your writing. You can be sure that you will always feel uncertain, so you may as well get used to it. Don't allow it to push you into making assumptions based on misinterpretations of partial facts of dubious value. Your writing is worth more than that.

Exercises

In your slogan journal, list all the times you have misinterpreted a situation because you didn't have the full picture.

Pick one of the situations on your list and explore what happened in detail. Why did you misinterpret what was going on? Were you misled by your feelings, your thinking, circumstances? What were the consequences of your misinterpretation?

Knowing what you do now, explore alternative ways of looking at this situation. What have you learned from the experience? What would you do differently now?

Slogan 53: Don't wobble

This slogan is about being consistent with your mind training practice and not getting sidetracked by other things in your life or doubts about what you are doing.

The original slogan is: *"Don't vacillate,"* which draws your attention to the way your mind tends to get caught up in its own vortex, running in circles and driving you crazy. If you follow your mind, you will end up running in circles too. But this is the point of practising mind training – to stop the mind from vacillating.

When life is going well and you're feeling inspired, it's easy to motivate yourself to meditate and read books about the teachings and share your enthusiasm with others. But when you're struggling, either with your practice or in life generally, you start to have doubts about what you're doing. Perhaps your meditation technique is wrong, or you're not doing it enough, or maybe you should try a different practice. Perhaps you're just not as enthusiastic as you were when you first started. Or perhaps you're not getting the results you hoped for, or it's starting to get boring.

When you begin to doubt yourself it makes you question everything and that makes you doubt yourself even more. The doubt feeds on itself and leads to more doubt in a vicious cycle. Your mind goes in circles trying to work out what to do and worrying itself silly. But too much thinking in this way drains your energy and self-confidence.

This slogan encourages you to stay with your practice through all its ups and downs, the successes and the failures. You won't feel the same way about it all the time – your energy levels and enthusiasm will change, just as with the rest of your life. But when you practice consistently it helps your mind to settle into positive habits that support your practice, and this can become a virtuous cycle.

Meditation is hard because you're trying to stop the mind from doing what it tends to do naturally. Thinking, weighing alternatives, testing theories, and worrying over things you can't control. You think like this because you're trying to avoid the present moment. When you come into the present, you may find yourself confronted by feelings and tensions you think you can't handle, so your mind spins off into questions and doubt. But the only way to deal with these feelings and tensions is to feel and accept them.

So this slogan reminds you to stay present and deal with reality instead of hiding inside your doubt. Make a decision. Either meditate or don't, but if you decide to do it, then get on with it and let go of the doubt. Your energy and enthusiasm will return when you get on with doing what you know, deep down, you need to do.

Commit to being consistent and don't wobble.

For Writers

Doubt is a way of life for writers. It's impossible to write anything without immediately worrying that it's not good enough or that you haven't expressed yourself clearly enough or that you might be wasting your time. Writing well takes time and energy and there will be days when you just can't face it. But as we've seen, too much doubt can be destructive, and if you let your doubts take over, your writing will suffer as much as you do.

It's much easier for doubt to get out of control if there are long periods in which you don't write. Other tasks and responsibilities seem to multiply and your writing gets lost in the rush. You may even believe yourself when you think the story idea you had was silly and that if you had written it down, it wouldn't have worked anyway. Besides, who are you to think you can write?

You have to nip that sort of pernicious thinking in the bud before it poisons your entire outlook on life. This slogan gives you a way to counter your mind's tendency to drive you up the wall. When you do something consistently it trains your mind to fall into a pattern. So if you consistently doubt your ability to write, you will be more likely to continue doing so, and less likely to write anything.

To train your mind to take your writing seriously and stop with the crazy making doubts, you need to practice writing consistently. Set aside a period of time every day when you can write without being disturbed and make sure you do it. Sticking to a schedule will train your mind to settle into writing on cue, exactly how Pavlov's dogs were trained to salivate when he rang a bell before feeding them. After a while the poor mutts would drool whenever a bell was rung.

Finding time to write may be a challenge, but it's not impossible if you are committed to taking your writing seriously. You may need to reorganise your schedule so you can focus on your priorities. But if you commit to doing this you must keep doing it. Don't set yourself up to fail by making your writing schedule impossible to maintain. And don't use your day job or family as excuses to avoid writing.

If you're struggling with doubt, you only need to make sure you write for a minimum of ten minutes every day, and you must do this consistently regardless how you feel about it. At first you might think it's pointless, but gradually, if you keep trying to write at the allotted time, it will get easier. Before you know it, your enthusiasm will return and you'll be writing for longer and longer and you won't be able to stop.

So be consistent and keep writing, but above all, remember this Zen proverb:

> *"In walking, just walk. In sitting, just sit. Above all, don't wobble."*

You could also add, "*In writing, just write.*"

Exercises

If you don't already have one, make a realistic writing schedule and stick to it. Make sure you write for at least 10 minutes every day.

In your slogan journal, make a list of all the ways you doubt yourself and/or your writing.

Pick your top five doubts and explore further. Why do you doubt yourself? Where does the doubt come from? Is the doubt realistic or are you beating yourself up over nothing? How could you put your doubt to the test?

Slogan 54: Be wholehearted

This slogan is about overcoming your defences and making a commitment to practice mind training wholeheartedly. The original slogan is: *"Train wholeheartedly,"* which means you don't avoid feelings or experiences that make you uncomfortable.

When you commit to training your mind, you can't make excuses or look for ways to avoid practising. It's not just another chore to do on your list, something to get through and then move onto the next thing. This slogan tells you to not be half-hearted. Meditation isn't a chore. It's something to put your whole being into.

To do that you must open your heart and that means being willing to feel whatever is there, and to soften towards yourself and life. Being wholehearted means dissolving the ego and allowing yourself to be changed, moved, and transformed by what you encounter. You have to be willing to be vulnerable, and to be hurt.

It's this human fragility that the ego tries to protect by forming a hard shell around your heart and mind. You live inside the battlements of this shell, the Ego Fort, the defensive structure of the ego that we saw in Slogan 19. When anything happens that threatens your sense of self or feelings of security, your ego starts to throw offensive weapons over the battlements at your enemies. You retreat further behind the thick walls that you have built and your life slowly ossifies.

The ego tenses up against the reality it doesn't like, or frantically chases what it believes will make it safer and stronger. Either way, it makes you miserable and cuts you off from the flow of life. But this is why you practice meditation – to pierce holes in the battlements and ultimately tear down the entire stinking edifice.

However, you don't go about this demolition process with grim determination and clenched fists. It's not a battle to the death, although it is sometimes portrayed that way in the spiritual literature. In the end, the best way to pull down your Ego Fort is to relax, watch the games the ego plays, keep your heart open and slowly the defensive structures will dissolve.

So there's no need to fear whatever lurks behind the quivering walls of your ego. When you catch yourself making excuses or trying to avoid practising, it may be a sign that your defences have been breached. But this is a good thing. Anything and everything that happens in your life can be used in your meditation practice. No matter what you're feeling, you can open your heart to it and allow it to slowly transform you.

For Writers

If you are following the advice of the previous slogan and practising your writing consistently every day, there will be times when you just don't feel like doing it. Perhaps you're tired or distracted by other responsibilities, or the piece you're working on feels stale. You've run out of inspiration and the last thing you want to do is force yourself to write something. If you write anyway, it feels like every word is wrenched from your mind with bolt cutters.

This slogan reminds you to approach your writing wholeheartedly, so when your enthusiasm wanes or you're struggling to motivate yourself, it's a sign that you need to dig a little deeper to find out what is going on. Don't make excuses or look for ways to avoid writing. And don't just write anyway, forcing the words out because you think you have to get it done.

If you want to write wholeheartedly you need to be honest with yourself about how you feel. Writing shouldn't be another chore on your list, so don't treat it like one. You either want to do it or you don't, so if you don't want to write today, ask yourself why.

Are you tired? If so, perhaps you need to take a break, get an early night and come back to your writing tomorrow ready to start again. Are you struggling to meet a deadline and feeling overwhelmed? If so, perhaps you need to renegotiate the deadline or delegate some other tasks to give you more time. Have you lost interest in the work? If so, perhaps you need to revisit the original inspiration for the piece, try approaching it from a fresh angle, or write something else.

There are many reasons why you might lose energy and focus in your writing, and the remedy for each will depend upon the problem.

Whatever is going on, don't beat yourself up for having difficulties, but see it as an opportunity to reconnect with your purpose.

The worst thing you can do is be half-hearted towards your writing. This stops you going deep into difficult emotions because you're probably avoiding them in yourself, hiding behind your battlements. Your writing will reflect your defensive attitude, and if you keep avoiding these difficult emotions you may have trouble creating fully rounded characters or convincing storylines. When your heart isn't in your work, you can't hide it and readers will feel your lack of care in every word you write.

This slogan asks you to be wholehearted. You can't do that if you're denying your own feelings and disconnected from your own experience. Writing is a practice that can bring you back to yourself and your real emotions. When you reconnect with your true Self by focusing on the present moment, you come back to life and your writing will reflect that natural energy and enthusiasm.

So say yes to this moment. Take a deep breath and come back to your body. Feel your heart beating in your chest, feel the blood rushing through your limbs. You are alive. Now write!

Exercises

In your slogan journal, explore the ways you have lost enthusiasm for your writing in the past, or now. Is there a pattern? Why do you stop caring?

Find a piece of writing you have completed that reflects this loss of heart. Find another piece of your writing that bursts with energy and life. Compare the two and make a note of the differences. What can you learn about yourself and your writing from these examples?

When you sit down to write every day, take a moment to breathe deeply and connect with your body. Feel your heart beating and say yes to your writing.

Slogan 55: Examine and analyse

This slogan is about examining how you are progressing with your mind training and analysing how you can continue to improve. The original slogan is: "*Liberate yourself by examining and analysing,*" and it turns the previous slogan on its head. Instead of dissolving your problems by opening your heart, this slogan asks you to think about and analyse them in great detail.

The idea is to examine and analyse your defensive ego patterns and difficult emotions. Think through why you do what you do, feel what you feel, and think the way you think. Doing this helps you to be honest with yourself about what is happening and makes it easier to see situations more clearly because you are less likely to fool yourself.

Deconstructing and examining your feelings and behaviour stops you from falling into the trap we saw in Slogan 52 where you avoid dealing with difficult emotions by floating off into a spiritual fantasy world. To be sure you're not fooling yourself, you need to watch the way your ego builds its defences so you can see how and why your negative habits arise. Because if you don't fully understand these defensive patterns you won't know if you have overcome them.

If you perform a spiritual bypass to avoid feeling the darker emotions that are part of being fully human, you're likely to experience a backlash at some point further down· the path. You can't fake awakening – you're either free of suffering or you're not. Lying to yourself about what you're feeling won't help you in the long run. You need to be honest with yourself so you can see which thoughts, feelings and actions lead to freedom, and which ones lead to more suffering.

This slogan encourages you to think about the things that make you feel defensive and unsure of yourself. Look into what makes you anxious, scared, angry, and resentful, but also look at what makes you too sure of yourself and overconfident. Watch how you swing back and forth between these extremes, convinced you're right one day, and then riddled with doubt the next.

It might seem like all you're doing is thinking about yourself when you do this, but if you ask the right questions and then act on the answers, it will help you to free yourself from the negative patterns that keep you locked in self-centred thinking and emotions. But it only works if you are honest with yourself.

Begin by watching yourself to see what is happening, and then analyse it. Ask yourself questions and keep digging until you get to the bottom of what you are doing and why. Is it a real problem or are you imagining things? How are you undermining yourself by retreating into your Ego Fort? Meditate on whatever comes up and open yourself to change.

Remember that your negative habits work best when they stay hidden behind the walls of your defensive structures, so this slogan tells you to force down the door, march in there and have a proper look around. The more you see what's really going on, the more you'll want to change. Then the easier it will be to allow the meditation to do its work.

For Writers

Writers spend an inordinate amount of time thinking about motivations. You need to understand why your characters choose certain actions over others in order to create believable subtext and storylines. So you are probably quite used to the kind of questioning this slogan demands. However, you might not be so diligent in applying this technique to yourself.

This slogan encourages you to constantly assess your progress and check in with yourself to see how you're doing. It's designed to focus your attention on what's important and keep you on track so you don't drift along, oblivious to what you're doing. Asking the right questions will help you notice when things aren't going the way you want, and to make the necessary adjustments to your path. This will stop you from wandering in circles and repeating yourself.

There are two ways to do this. One is to apply it to yourself to help you unearth habits that interfere with your writing. The other is to apply it to the writing itself to deconstruct your stories and check that they work, and ensure that you're not writing the same story over and over.

When applying this slogan to yourself, the first thing you need is to be as honest with yourself as you can. Take a good look at your life and your habits. Is everything working the way you would like, or are there areas you would like to improve? Do you struggle to write as much as you would like, or do you keep getting stuck? Don't be too quick to assume that everything is fine. There could be something lurking behind the walls of your Ego Fort that is subtly undermining you without your knowledge.

Once you have located the problem (or problems), ask appropriate questions and listen for the answers. Write the entire process down in your notebook and allow your answers to flow spontaneously without censoring yourself. Define the situation and ask what you can do to change it. Look into why you doubt yourself so much, for example. Do you give up too easily? Why do you get stuck? Is it always the same problems? Why?

If you can't change the situation, can you learn to accept it? Can you let it go? Do you need help or support?

You can learn a lot about yourself by examining and analysing your writing and asking the right questions. Not only will you release yourself from bad habits that hold you back, but being honest with yourself will also help to keep your writing fresh. You can't express yourself freely when you're hiding behind the walls of your Ego Fort. Kick down the door with a few impertinent questions.

Exercises

In your slogan journal, explore your writing by answering these questions:

- Why did you create these particular characters? How are they like you and how are they different? What can you learn from this?

- Which are your favourite characters, and are there any you don't like? What can you learn from this?

- Why did you tell these particular stories? Do the same themes and issues keep coming up? What can you learn from this?

- Is there a subject you always avoid? Why?

- Are you stuck in your writing? Why?

- Do you avoid getting feedback on your writing? Do you send your work out? If not, why? What are you scared of?

Add any other questions you need to answer.

Slogan 56: Don't wallow

This slogan is about not letting your darker feelings drag you under, especially when things don't go your way or your meditation practice becomes more challenging. The original slogan is: "*Don't wallow in self-pity,*" which reminds you not to feel sorry for yourself, no matter what you're going through.

If you have been examining and analysing your negative habits and digging up all the ways you make things worse for yourself and others, there may be times when you wish you had never started poking around in your mind trying to change things. You might even believe you were better off before you took up this meditation nonsense! Sometimes it's just too much hard work and you wish you could give up and go back to sleep. But this slogan gives you a sharp prod and reminds you not to wallow in self-pity.

All this complaining about how hard it is or how meditation is boring, is just another ego tactic of avoidance and denial. When things are going badly, it's easy to get caught in self-pity. This is especially true when you uncover some of the darker sides of yourself, such as painful experiences and emotions like shame, self-hatred, self-recrimination, and depression.

This slogan reminds you to work with these feelings of darkness and despair rather than turning them into an excuse to wallow. When you catch yourself feeling self-pity it means your ego is trying to get you to run back inside its fort and pull up the drawbridge. But don't give in to the despair. If you do, you'll notice that it increases your suffering and isolates you even more.

Instead, turn your darkest feelings into the object of your meditation practice. You can examine and analyse your feelings to determine where they come from and why. Or you can practice tonglen by breathing in your self-pity and despair, and breathing out compassion.

Life is hard and depressing at times. Things don't always go the way you hope and you end up holding the shitty end of the stick. But if you hang on to the stick and complain about how you're holding it, and yet refuse to drop the stick, well, who is to blame for that? Let go of the stick!

You're not the only one who is struggling. It's hard being human and suffering is universal. Use this fact to open your heart to compassion, not to drown in self-pity.

You can undercut the entire problem by asking one question: Who is feeling sorry for themselves? See if you can find the self who is wallowing (clue: it doesn't inherently exist) and you will be liberated.

For Writers

Stop me if you've heard this before, but writing is hard. This fact bears repeating because writers sometimes forget that what they're trying to do is actually quite difficult. You are attempting to capture reality in words, a reality that is elusive and mysterious and prone to change without warning.

When you sit down to write, regardless how many times you have done it before or how successful you have been up to that point, you have no idea what you're doing. You don't know if you're wasting your time. You don't know if you're deluding yourself. You may well be, but you do know that if you don't write you will feel terrible, so you do it anyway.

However, there will be times when the doubt becomes too much and the impossibility of what you're trying to achieve will crush your spirit. When that happens, you stop writing. What you do next is crucial.

Do you give in to the doubt and wallow in self-pity?

This slogan reminds you that it's natural to struggle at times, but that doesn't mean you have to torture yourself over it. When you focus on how hard writing is and how difficult it can be to achieve your goals, you will never enjoy the process of writing. If you haven't written for a while and you spend more time beating yourself up than you spend actually writing, it may be time step back and look at what you're doing to yourself.

Why are you tormenting yourself? If the problem stems from your feelings about yourself, then you need to practice self-acceptance and tonglen until you clear the negativity enough to get your pen moving again. If the problem stems from your feelings about the writing itself, then you need to examine and analyse your work to find a solution.

However, if the problem stems from more abstract fears about how hard it is to write well or to sell your work, you may need to have a closer look at your expectations. No matter how much writing you do, it will never get any easier. You will just have to accept it and get on with it.

So don't wallow in self-pity. All it does it make you feel bad and that makes writing even harder – and it's hard enough already.

Exercises

In your slogan journal, list all the times you have given into to self-pity. If you never have, good for you! (But I suspect you may be in denial – have another think...)

Pick one of the situations from your list and explore it in more depth. Why did you react with self-pity? How did you stop yourself from wallowing? What did you learn from this experience?

Examine your expectations. Do they support your desire to write and share your work? Or do they undermine you?

Slogan 57: Don't be jealous

This slogan is about remembering not to be jealous of others. The original slogan is the same and it encourages you to pay attention to how you compare yourself with others, especially when you feel insecure.

Jealousy comes from a feeling of not having enough or not being good enough. Maybe you feel you never get what you deserve, despite trying your hardest. Other people are doing so much better, and you're stuck feeling sorry for yourself and brooding on the unfairness of it all. If you're not careful, this can get out of control and feed into self-pity and feelings of depression and hopelessness. It becomes a vicious circle. The more you notice how much better other people are, the worse you feel about yourself and the more jealous you become.

Jealousy can take many forms. Perhaps you crave more money, power, status, a big car, a beautiful home, more glamorous friends, talent, brains, and beauty. Jealousy can even infect your spiritual aspirations and drive you to want more profound spiritual experiences, more awakenings, insight, wisdom, better posture in yoga class, or the ability to meditate for hours. The list of possibilities is endless.

Comparing yourself to others in this way makes no sense because everybody has different needs and values. Even if you succeed in getting all the things you covet, the chances are they won't make you happier or more secure, or whatever it is you think you need. When you let jealousy take over your life, all it does is undermine your own self-belief and confidence. It stops you from appreciating what you already have and the many positive qualities you possess.

This slogan challenges you to work with your jealousy so you can transform it into gratitude. Pay attention to all the small moments of jealousy that you experience and examine why you might be reacting the way you do. Ask yourself what you believe you lack, and look deeply into yourself to see if it's true. If it is true, see if there's anything you can do about it. If there isn't anything to be done, can you accept the situation as it is?

For example, if you're jealous of people who have more money than you, perhaps it's because you don't have enough money. If that's true and you can't pay your bills, then feeling jealous isn't going to help you find the money you need. But if you can pay your bills and you still want more cash, then you need to look a little deeper to discover the real cause of your jealousy. Perhaps you're just being greedy, or maybe you're scared of losing what you have because you're insecure.

Ultimately, this is about self-acceptance. Feeling jealous of others is a way to hide from your fears and insecurity, so this slogan encourages you to accept yourself as you are. Be kinder to yourself and remember all your positive qualities. You can also flip jealousy on its head and practice feeling joy for others who are happy and successful.

We're all interconnected so increasing the amount of happiness in the world will benefit everyone. Accepting yourself will help others to accept themselves, and feeling gratitude for the happiness you see in others will reduce your own suffering. Your happiness becomes my happiness in a virtuous circle of joy.

For Writers

All writers fantasise about achieving runaway success with their work at some point in their careers. Perhaps you dream of selling millions of copies of your latest novel, or winning a prestigious book prize and being lauded as a genius, or the next whoever. There's nothing wrong with this fantasy as long as you don't take it too seriously. But if you start to believe this dream too fervently you will make yourself and everybody around you miserable.

Achieving success as a writer depends on multiple conditions all coming together at once, most of which you have little or no control over. Not only that, but stratospheric levels of success are extremely rare, and most writers depend on a day job to pay their bills. Which is why jealousy is rampant in writers. They may not admit it, but scratch the skin of the average writer and you will find a seething green pit of envy.

This slogan reminds you that feeling jealousy isn't in your best interest. When you compare your level of success or talent with other writers, you undermine your ability to see your own writing clearly. There may be nothing wrong with the way you write, but if you constantly compare it against others, especially those who appear to be more successful, you will start to believe you're not good enough.

Comparing your writing with that of others can be useful if you do it in the spirit of learning how to improve your work. You can pick up tips for making your prose more dynamic or for creating believable dialogue. You can even learn the skills you need to sell your work more effectively by studying the techniques used to attract readers.

But if you allow your inspiration to sour into jealousy because you feel bitter about your lack of success, your writing will suffer and so will you. So when you feel tempted to give in to the green-eyed monster, take a step back and notice what you're doing. It may be true that the object of your jealousy is a better writer or more successful, but instead of hating them for it, ask yourself what you can learn from them.

When you see another writer achieve fabulous success, great plaudits and mountains of cash, be pleased for them. Be inspired. It shows what is possible if you work hard on your writing and create something for readers to enjoy. Be grateful for the opportunity to read their work and learn from them. Doing this will help to reduce the amount of jealousy you feel and inspire you to try harder with your own writing.

Exercises

In your slogan journal, make a list of all the people who make you feel jealous. Use a green pen, just for fun.

Examine your list and see if you can spot any patterns. What do you crave? What qualities do you secretly admire?

Analyse the things you envy to discover how you really feel about yourself. What do you fear you lack? Explore your feelings about this.

Pick an author you admire/envy and find out more about their life before they achieved fame and fortune. Does this make you admire or envy them more or less? What can you learn from this?

Slogan 58: Don't be frivolous

This slogan is about finding the right balance between joy and seriousness, and focusing on the things that really matter you. The original slogan is the same and, on face value, seems to be telling you to not have any fun. But thankfully there's more to it than that. It's asking you to look more deeply at how you spend your time and the kinds of things you care about.

When you are being frivolous you don't really let anything touch you deeply. It can feel like fun to skate over the surface of life being silly and having a laugh. But when you live like this all the time it's hard to make meaningful choices or commit to anything for very long.

Being frivolous can be a way to avoid confronting feelings or ideas that make you uncomfortable or force you to change. It takes effort to avoid the depths and stop your scary emotions from erupting and spoiling the fun. Frivolity then becomes a kind of denial. The silliness and larking about are really a desperate attempt to cheer yourself up and convince yourself that everything is fine.

But this doesn't mean you have to be serious all the time and never have fun or enjoy yourself. It's just that real joy and happiness come from a deeper place than frivolity. You can tell when joyful behaviour isn't genuine because it has an edge, a manic determination, as if you're forcing yourself to have as much fun as possible, whatever the cost.

Real joy is infectious; it draws people closer and opens hearts. To feel joy you need to be at peace with yourself, not avoiding your feelings or fighting against yourself. In other words, if you're functioning through your ego then you can't feel real joy because you're too defended and insecure.

But if you catch yourself being frivolous, don't compensate by becoming deadly serious instead. It's not about swinging to the opposite extreme. This slogan isn't telling you to be serious. It's saying don't be shallow. Don't hide from your depths. Don't waste your time on things that don't make you feel more alive and present and awake.

Real joy is a spontaneous expression of your true Buddha nature. When you focus on your intention to wake up, this slogan can bring you back into alignment with your natural playfulness and remind you that life is too short for superficial nonsense.

For Writers

One of the biggest problems you face as a writer, and one of the most predictable excuses, is that you don't have time to write. Without giving it much thought, you're convinced that because you spend your days knee-deep in frenetic doing that you couldn't possibly squeeze in another half hour of so-called 'free time.' But this is probably a lie.

How long do you spend surfing the internet? Perhaps you're glued to your computer screen or phone because you're researching an important subject that you want to write about. Or maybe you're just looking at pictures of cats. Or reading click-bait. Or posting outraged tweets about things of which you know nothing. Or creating fun memes to cheer up your friends.

Distraction doesn't have to come via the internet. There are so many ways to kill time with frivolous eyewash that it has become an industry in itself. Frivolity has been normalised and monetised and turned into a way of life, and this is what makes it dangerous to writers. It's dangerous to everybody, but writers and other creative folk need to be particularly careful to protect their time. It's too easy to become enthralled by the shallow clamouring of the culture in which you're embedded, and this can have a disastrous effect on your ability to be truly creative.

If you want to write then you have to actually do some writing, but you also need time to think and find inspiration and percolate ideas. To others it looks like writers are wasting time doing not much of anything – sitting about reading novels, daydreaming, relaxing, watching movies, staring out of the window and letting your imagination run wild. But this is productive idleness, and you can't be creative without it.

This presents a problem. You already have limited time available, so how do you choose where to put your attention? This slogan encourages you to pay attention to how you are spending your time and to think about the effect this has on your ability to write the way you want.

If your cultural inspiration comes from too superficial a level, you'll just regurgitate what you're fed and have nothing new to say. Nobody wants to read the same stories over and over. Books and movies and TV dramas can inspire you, but you don't need all the fluff that surrounds them – the endless opinion and pontificating and dissection.

Allow your inspiration to come from deep inside and let the inputs from your culture work on you in silence. Don't allow your feelings about the culture to be shaped by the opinion of sheep and people who are chasing advertising revenue. Think and process ideas for yourself. You do have time to write. You don't have time for shallow cultural offerings that leave you feeling dead inside.

This isn't an argument against 'low art.' One man's offal is another man's sweetbread, and where you find inspiration is irrelevant as long as you know how to engage with it deeply. In other words, you need to have serious fun.

Serious fun is productive idleness. It is having fun mindfully with the intention of enriching your creative work. So when you have fun, be present with your experience. Don't beat yourself up with guilt thinking you should be working or doing something more important. Inspiration is important. It fuels your imagination and without it, you won't write a word.

But if you are being frivolous and wasting your time on mindless distractions, be honest with yourself and stop. Nobody needs another Lolcat.

Exercises

In your slogan journal, list your favourite ways of having fun.

Boost your creativity by making space for productive idleness in your life. Rethink your schedule to include downtime and room for fun.

In your slogan journal, list the frivolous distractions you could live without.

Make a commitment to banish at least one of your frivolities forever. You can only cross it off your list when you have successfully not indulged in it for at least two months.

Slogan 59: Don't expect applause

This slogan is about not expecting recognition or applause for the things you do. The original slogan is the same and it encourages you to let go of attachment to the outcome, in a similar way to Slogan 28.

Nobody in their right mind expects applause for practising mind training and meditation. You know you're not going to be recognised for your amazing ability to stay focused on the present moment. But you may be surprised how subtle your need for recognition can be. So this slogan asks you to pay attention to your desire for approval and appreciation.

For example, do you expect to be thanked when you help somebody? Notice how you react when you don't receive the appreciation you think you deserve. Perhaps you feel aggrieved or mildly offended, and think the other person has rejected you or is being ungrateful. Perhaps you believe that because you express gratitude when others help you, that they should return the favour.

But this slogan says you can't do that. You can't hold others up to your personal standards or values because that is a subtle form of control. You can't force others to behave or feel the way you want. It's good to be thankful and to appreciate the good that others do, but you can't expect that appreciation for yourself.

This is because it's not about you. If you help others because you want to be appreciated for it, then you're more interested in being recognised as a good person than in actually doing good. When you expect applause for something you have done, you're doing things in expectation of a specific result, but you can't control the outcome. You can't control how others will react.

When you do things with the expectation of getting something in return it distorts your perception of what's important. You put the cart before the horse and start chasing things that deliver greater recognition – money, power, success, and fame – because those things will make you more visible. Then everything you do becomes about getting attention rather than doing something valuable or worthwhile or even enjoyable.

Needing recognition and applause makes you dependent on what others think of you, and this is not a happy place to be. When you put your need for recognition above everything else, you give others the power to make or break you. Your happiness is in their hands.

Expecting applause for being spiritual makes no sense. You won't be congratulated for becoming a saint, especially if you secretly hope you will. Compassion and meditation are not spectator sports. You don't meditate to win medals. You do it to be calm and focused and to reconnect with your deeper Self and feel more alive. You don't need applause for that. Feeling alive is reward enough in itself.

So enjoy the appreciation you receive when you get it, but don't expect it or let it go to your head. You don't need applause for meditating every day. You just sit and breathe. It's no big deal.

For Writers

Most people think writers are weird. Maybe they are, or maybe they're just human. But whatever the truth, non-writers have very little appreciation for the work that goes into writing a novel. To make matters worse, unless you become insanely successful, many people won't even believe you're a writer. If you have a day job, and most writers do, then as far as the average person is concerned, you're not a writer.

This means you're unlikely to be congratulated just for writing something. It doesn't matter how long it takes, or how hard you work, or the care with which you craft your story, if you expect applause you will be disappointed. And if you need applause and recognition in order to feel motivated, you're likely to give up writing altogether.

The desire to seek approval will disrupt your ability to write because it leaves you open to manipulation by others. It also hands too much power to your own fears because chasing recognition and success is often compensation for a feeling of lack in other areas. So rather than dealing with your doubt and lack of self-worth, you try to prove yourself worthy by filling your life with accomplishments and trophies.

But no amount of fame and fortune will make you feel better about yourself. In fact, you may feel even worse because, on top of the low self-esteem, you'll feel like a fraud or an imposter. The more desperate your need for outer approval, the more desperate you'll feel inside.

When it comes to navigating the minefield of publishing, whether you take the traditional route or do it yourself, this is the question you will have to answer: Do you stay true to your ideas and your vision, or do you write for the market? Your response will depend on your intention and what you hope to achieve with your writing. But this slogan may give you pause. Don't be too quick to sell out.

It makes no difference whether you stay true to your own voice or follow the latest market trends; you may or may not be successful, either way. There's no guarantee you will receive the recognition you crave. But if you compromise on your ideas and your voice, and you happen to achieve success, it may feel hollow because you betrayed your values. On the other hand, if you fail despite having compromised, you'll feel bitter and may blame others for your failure.

You will have to decide for yourself whether it's worth betraying your values and handing over power to something you can't control. Of course, it's perfectly possible to stay true to your own voice and write for the market, if those two happen to coincide. It's also possible to be wildly successful by bucking all market trends and blowing everyone's minds. This is because nobody knows what will sell.

You are better off concentrating on writing the best story you can, regardless what anybody else thinks or what happens to be selling this week. You have to be true to yourself because that is all you have. And nobody can take that away from you, even if you fail in spectacular fashion.

Writing, like meditation, is about the process. It's great when others appreciate your work, but don't rely on it. Audiences are fickle and the next thing you write might be lucky to elicit a shrug.

Write because not writing is impossible. Write to explore, to discover yourself, surprise yourself, scare yourself, confront yourself, to learn, laugh, cry, and live. Just don't expect applause.

Exercises

In your slogan journal, explore your motivation for writing. Write for as long as it takes to unearth how you really feel.

Now explore your feelings about success. What does success mean to you? What would you be willing to do to achieve success?

Now explore how you feel about receiving recognition for your writing. How do you feel when others don't like your work? Are you defensive? Defiant? Indifferent? Devastated?

Indulge in a little fantasy: Imagine your latest book is a runaway success. Think through the implications for your work. What would you be expected to do now that you're a successful author? Could you repeat your success? Can you live up to the expectations of your publisher, agent, and readers?

Final Thoughts

Writing and meditation appear to be opposites. In meditation you turn inwards and relax into the peace of your true Self. In writing you externalise your mind and bring forth what is inside to create something new. Meditation is silence; writing is a cacophony of voices. But these differences are only apparent.

Both meditation and writing are about self-exploration and encourage you to open your heart to experience as it is lived. Both require a willingness to be changed by what you discover, and both demand a level of humility that can be challenging. Neither work well from within the confines of the Ego Fort. Writing and meditation succeed when you get out of your own way and allow the moment to be what it is.

The present moment reveals the awareness at the root of all experience, a still point at the centre of a swirling vortex of change. You are caught in this vortex, trying your best to make sense of your life as it flashes past. Perhaps this is why you write. To record your experience, so fleeting and ephemeral, to catch it before it evaporates into the void.

You take ownership of the ephemeral stuff of life when you reflect upon experience and tell your story. Through the act of imagination, the impersonal is transformed into the personal. But life isn't really about you. All the desires, hopes and dreams that feel so personal, are actually collective. We all get scared and angry, and fall in love and make fools of ourselves. But in our hearts, we are one.

The true purpose of storytelling is alchemy. As you tell your story, you create yourself. You create your soul.

There's an African saying, *"God created man because he likes to hear stories."* In other words, the universe, life, God, or whatever you want to call it, uses you in order to explore itself. Your story is how the universe comes to know itself.

You are one tiny strand of divine thought spinning stories about yourself as you try to find your way home, back to where you already are.

It all comes down to this combination of the ego and the Self, the animal and the Divine, being and non-being. Somehow, when these two worlds meet they create a human being, and the mystery of life is bound up with the question of what it means to be human. And what it means to be you.

There seems to be an evolutionary imperative at work in human consciousness. Life is always growing and seeking out new frontiers. It is ruthless in its pursuit of more life, more consciousness, more experience. The driving force behind this is love – the only force powerful enough to counter entropy and death. Love is always transgressive and ultimately, completely impersonal.

You build walls. Love tears them down. You create barriers in your mind against the truth. Love turns them to fire and ash.

Life wants you to evolve. It wants you to live, fully and joyfully. It wants to know itself and play through you.

Who are you to stand in its way?

What happens next?

We have reached the end of the book. Have you been meditating? Have you been writing? Are you still making excuses?

> *"If you want to meditate there is virtually no excuse not to. But human confusion is very clever, so it is still possible to talk yourself out of it. If so, be my guest. Sometimes that's the way to finally begin serious meditation practice: by not doing it for ten or twenty years, until finally there is no choice."* – Norman Fischer, *Training in Compassion*

Read the above quote again and substitute writing for meditation. **If you want to write there is no excuse not to**. If you want to write you will have to make it as much a part of your life as every other essential. You wouldn't go a day without eating or sleeping. Writing should be the same. It's part of the fabric of who you are, so give it the space and time it deserves. You would starve if you didn't eat. What will happen to your soul if you don't write?

I can't make you write. I can't scale the walls of your Ego Fort and fire pellets of freedom at you over the battlements. You will have to do that yourself. But I do know that the process outlined in this book works, if you put it into practice.

If you would like to go further and explore the slogans in more depth, the appendix includes a glossary of terms and a list of the original slogans, as well as reference books on lojong and online resources, plus useful books on writing and creativity. You may also like to visit the slogan randomiser at **Lojong for Writers**.

I hope this book will be of benefit to you. It helped me to write it, and I hope it helps you too.

May your pen and your mind be free!

Appendix

Glossary of Terms

Awareness

When we talk about Awareness in the context of Buddhist teachings, we mean something quite specific. It's not just the conscious mind or your perception of what's happening, although it includes those things. Awareness is the background, the Source or Ground of all life. It contains everything and is nothing.

Awareness can also be called Emptiness, Suchness, Pure Awareness, No-mind, Oneness, Non-duality Consciousness, Brahman, Original Mind, Buddha Mind, and God. Awareness is variously described as Undifferentiated, Unborn, Unchanging, Limitless, and Eternal. It is Universal, Collective, Transpersonal or Impersonal, Empty, Void, Non-being, and No-thingness.

> "This state cannot be seen because it is everything seen, and so remains Unshown. It cannot be heard, because it is everything heard, and so remains Unspeakable. It cannot be known, because it is everything known, and so remains Great Mystery." – Ken Wilber, The Atman Project

The existence of Awareness can't be proved because there is nothing outside of it. You can't get beyond Awareness to verify or measure it because you are it. You are Awareness, but you tend to split your experience of it into a subject and an object. You believe the world is made up of separate objects because that is how it looks, and you even turn yourself into another object in consciousness. But when you look for this self, try to pin it down and interrogate it – it disappears. The self morphs into the Self, fades into the background, opens into nothingness and is gone.

At the level of Awareness, all of existence is one. This doesn't mean that everything is literally one, and that it's all somehow joined together in a big amorphous gloop, a random chaos of stuff that your brain conveniently sorts out into manageable, separate objects. It means Awareness is emptiness.

Try this thought experiment: In reality, there is only one Mind, which is non-dual Awareness, expressing itself through 7.5 billion different perspectives. Imagine looking through 7.5 billion pairs of eyes simultaneously. What would you see? If you really want to blow your mind, include all the animals, birds, and insects too...

See also: Buddha Mind, and Shunyata

Bodhicitta

Bodhicitta means 'enlightened or awakened mind and heart.' There are two types of bodhicitta, absolute and relative, although the distinction really only exists in your mind. **Absolute bodhicitta** is the foundation of wisdom and goodness, the ground of all existence, and **Relative bodhicitta** is that wisdom and goodness put into action in the world. Relative bodhicitta arises from absolute bodhicitta, so in reality, they are the same. You experience relative bodhicitta as compassion and love, while absolute bodhicitta is your perception of pure awareness before it manifests in action.

Absolute bodhicitta can also be called emptiness or shunyata. It is your true nature, or Buddha mind, and is the ultimate reality. It is the groundless ground of all being and exists beyond concepts. Absolute bodhicitta is awareness before is becomes split into subject and object in your mind. Relative bodhicitta is what you do with this perception of the interdependent and interconnected nature of existence. It is love and compassion in action, and arises spontaneously when you realise there is no separation between you and others.

See also: Awareness, Buddha Mind, and Shunyata

Buddha Mind

Buddha mind is your true nature, and it exists as the potential for enlightenment in all sentient beings. It's usually called Buddha nature, or *Buddha-dhātu*, which is a Sanskrit word meaning 'Buddha Element' or 'Buddha Principle.' Buddha nature is the ground of your being and the inherent nature of all manifest things. Knowledge of Buddha nature is your birthright because it is who you are at the most fundamental level. It is pure Awareness, or emptiness, effortlessly aware, clear and spacious. The entire universe is an expression of Buddha nature.

> *"Therefore, the very impermanency of grass and tree, thicket and forest is the Buddha nature. The very impermanency of men and things, body and mind, is the Buddha nature. Nature and lands, mountain and rivers, are impermanent because they are the Buddha nature. Supreme and complete enlightenment, because it is impermanent, is the Buddha nature."* – Heinrich Dumoulin

Emptiness

See: Shunyata

Four Immeasurables

The Four Immeasurables are states of mind or being that can be cultivated through your meditation practice. These 'divine abodes' or virtues are boundless and arise from your true nature, or Buddha mind. The four immeasurables are loving-kindness, compassion, empathetic joy, and equanimity. By developing these qualities and seeking to spread them to others through your spiritual practice, you can gain freedom from suffering and help others to do the same. Practising the Four Immeasurables will lead to greater peace and tranquillity for everyone. Begin the dedication with yourself, and then practice for all beings using these lines:

May I have happiness and the causes of happiness
May I be free from suffering and the causes of suffering
May I never be separated from joy that is without suffering
May I abide in equanimity, free from attachment and hatred

May all sentient beings have happiness and the causes of happiness.
May all sentient beings be free from suffering and the causes of suffering.
May all sentient beings never be separated from joy without suffering.
May all sentient beings be in equanimity, free from attachment and hatred.

Kayas

Kayas means 'bodies.' The kayas represent the four aspects of being and show how emptiness manifests and how we experience it through the process of awakening. The four kayas are:

- Dharmakaya: the truth or dharma body
- Sambhogakaya: the bliss or enjoyment body
- Nirmanakaya: the form body
- Svabhavikakaya: the essential body

The **dharmakaya** is the space or emptiness from which everything arises. It is the true form of the Buddha, i.e. Buddha mind. The **sambhogakaya** is the energy or vibration as emptiness moves, i.e. the energetic component of your perception. In other words, not perception through the senses, but the actual felt experience of whatever you're perceiving, or its quality. The **nirmanakaya** is the form or appearance that emptiness takes when it manifests. Finally, the **svabhavikakaya** is the essence of all the other kayas and reveals how they manifest simultaneously in the present moment. So space, energy and appearance all arise together out of emptiness. For example, you can see how this works with sound:

- Silence (or pure awareness) = dharmakaya
- The vibration in the air = sambhogakaya
- The sound (your eardrum sends a signal to your brain, etc.) = nirmanakaya
- Your experience of the sound in the moment = svabhavikakaya

You can't hear the sound unless all three kayas are present. Your perception and the experience arise together out of emptiness. There's no real separation between inside and outside, subject and object. Listen to a clock ticking and ask yourself: Where is the sound? Is it inside or outside your head? Which comes first, the ticking or your perception of the ticking?

Shunyata

Shunyata is a Sanskrit word that is usually translated as '**emptiness**,' which is unfortunate because it's a little misleading to Western minds. Whatever you think emptiness means, it doesn't mean that nothing exists or that everything is just happening in your head and that nothing really matters. These confusions happen because you're trying to think about something that can't really be thought about. Emptiness can't be grasped by the intellect and can only be experienced directly. So what is emptiness?

To understand the nature of emptiness, you need to understand cause and effect. Everything that appears to exist arises due to various causes and conditions, but these causes also depend upon other causes, and so on. For example, to grow a plant you need a seed, but the seed comes from the plant. Also the seed won't grow without soil, water, and favourable conditions. Does the seed cause the plant? Does the plant cause the seed? A seed can't pop into existence on its own without cause, and neither can a plant.

Both the seed and the plant are said to be empty of inherent existence because they depend on each other in order to exist. To inherently exist a form would have to arise spontaneously from nothing without cause. So a cause can't exist before its result. And the result can't exist before its cause. Cause and result can't exist simultaneously. Therefore any form that arises due to causes and conditions, does not inherently exist. Its appearance is empty.

This applies to everything that arises, including your feelings, thoughts, and consciousness. It's instructive to look at opposites too, such as light and dark, clean and dirty, happiness and suffering. Which comes first? Can light exist without dark? What does up mean without down?

If something inherently existed it would have to exist on its own, objectively and without depending on anything else. It would have its own inherent nature. Since everything does depend on something else in order to exist, or appear, things don't have any inherent nature or existence. They are empty of true existence. So no thing can be said to truly exist.

This doesn't mean that nothing exists. It just means that everything depends on everything else in order to exist. Emptiness means there is no inherent identity. There is no self in me or you or anything else. The Buddha said, "*The eye is empty of the eye.*" In other words, the eye is empty of itself. It doesn't inherently exist because it depends on other things. So emptiness means no-thing-ness. There is no 'thing' that is separate from other 'things'. The true nature of reality is beyond all concepts, beyond existence and non-existence.

In fact, if things did exist and had their own inherent existence, nothing could arise. Emptiness is what makes everything possible. If reality wasn't empty of existence, then it wouldn't be able to exist!

> *"You could say that emptiness is an open-ended potential for any and all sorts of experience to appear or disappear – the way a crystal ball is capable of reflecting all sorts of colours because it is, in itself, free from any colour."* – Yongey Mingyur Rinpoche

This applies to emptiness too. Emptiness can only exist in relation to something that isn't empty. Empty and not empty exist in dependence on each other, so neither of them inherently exists.

You may be wondering why you need to worry about all this metaphysics, but this is the key to awakening. Happiness and suffering are the way things appear to be, but they are concepts. The true nature of reality transcends them both. This may be hard to accept when you're in the middle of an extreme experience, but suffering comes from clinging to the idea that things exist in a permanent way.

If suffering existed the way you believe it does, you could never be free of it because it would be your permanent nature – and that is impossible. Your true nature is free of all conditions. It is empty and glorious and always free.

Original Slogans

The Root Text of the Seven Points of Training the Mind
By Chekawa Yeshe Dorje

Point One:
The Preliminaries, Which Are a Basis for Dharma Practice
I prostrate to the Great Compassionate One

1. First, train in the preliminaries.

Point Two:
The Main Practice, Which Is Training in Bodhicitta
Absolute Bodhicitta

2. Regard all dharmas as dreams.
3. Examine the nature of unborn awareness.
4. Self-liberate even the antidote.
5. Rest in the nature of *alaya*, the essence.
6. In post-meditation, be a child of illusion.

Relative Bodhicitta

7. Sending and taking should be practiced alternately. These two should ride the breath.
8. Three objects, three poisons, and three seeds of virtue.
9. In all activities, train with slogans.
10. Begin the sequence of sending and taking with yourself.

Point Three:
Transformation of Bad Circumstances into the Path of Enlightenment

11. When the world is filled with evil, transform all mishaps into the path of *bodhi*.
12. Drive all blames into one.
13. Be grateful to everyone.
14. Seeing confusion as the four *kayas* is unsurpassable *shunyata* protection.
15. Four practices are the best of methods.
16. Whatever you meet unexpectedly, join with meditation.

Point Four:
Showing the Utilisation of Practice in One's Whole Life

17. Practice the five strengths; the condensed heart instructions.
18. The mahayana instruction for ejection of consciousness at death is the five strengths: how you conduct yourself is important.

Point Five:
Evaluation of Mind Training

19. All dharma agrees at one point.
20. Of the two witnesses, hold the principle one.
21. Always maintain only a joyful mind.
22. If you can practice even when distracted, you are well trained.

Point Six:
Disciplines of Mind Training

23. Always abide by the three basic principles.
24. Change your attitude, but remain natural.
25. Don't talk about injured limbs.
26. Don't ponder others.

27. Work with the greatest defilements first.

28. Abandon any hope of fruition.

29. Abandon poisonous food.

30. Don't be so predictable.

31. Don't malign others.

32. Don't wait in ambush.

33. Don't bring things to a painful point.

34. Don't transfer the ox's load to the cow.

35. Don't try to be the fastest.

36. Don't act with a twist.

37. Don't make gods into demons.

38. Don't seek others' pain as the limbs of your own happiness.

Point Seven:
Guidelines of Mind Training

39. All activities should be done with one intention.

40. Correct all wrongs with one intention.

41. Two activities: one at the beginning, one at the end.

42. Whichever of the two occurs, be patient.

43. Observe these two, even at the risk of your life.

44. Train in the three difficulties.

45. Take on the three principle causes.

46. Pay heed that the three never wane.

47. Keep the three inseparable.

48. Train without bias in all areas. It is crucial always to do this pervasively and wholeheartedly.

49. Always meditate on whatever provokes resentment.

50. Don't be swayed by external circumstances.

51. This time, practice the main points.

52. Don't misinterpret.

53. Don't vacillate.

54. Train wholeheartedly.

55. Liberate yourself by examining and analysing.

56. Don't wallow in self-pity.

57. Don't be jealous.

58. Don't be frivolous.

59. Don't expect applause.

> *When the five ages occur,*
> *This is the way to transform them into the path of bodhi.*
> *This is the essence of the amrita of the oral instructions,*
> *Which were handed down from the tradition of the sage of*
> *Suvarnadvipa.*
> *Having awakened the karma of previous training*
> *And being urged on by intense dedication,*
> *I disregarded misfortune and slander*
> *And received oral instruction on taming ego-fixation.*
> *Now, even at death, I will have no regrets.*

From *Start Where You Are* by Pema Chodron

References and Resources

Commentaries on the lojong slogans:

Always Maintain a Joyful Mind: and Other Lojong Teachings on Awakening Compassion and Fearlessness by Pema Chodron

Start Where You Are: A Guide to Compassionate Living by Pema Chodron

Enlightened Courage: An Explanation of Atisha's Seven Point Mind Training by Dilgo Khyentse Rinpoche

Training in Compassion: Zen Teachings on the Practice of Lojong by Norman Fischer

The Great Path of Awakening by Ken McLeod

The Seven Points of Mind Training by The Venerable Thrangu Rinpoche

The Practice of Lojong: Cultivating Compassion through Training the Mind by Traleg Kyabgon

Training the Mind and Cultivating Loving-Kindness by Chogyam Trungpa

Buddhism with an Attitude: The Tibetan Seven-Point Mind Training by Alan Wallace

Online Resources:

Lojong for Writers: lojongforwriters.wordpress.com
Slogan randomiser by the author

Study Buddhism: studybuddhism.com
Project of the Berzin Archives: practical and authentic Buddhist teachings from Tibet

The Seven Points of Mind Training - online version of the book by Thrangu Rinpoche: www.rinpoche.com/teachings/sevenpoints.htm

Unfettered Mind: unfetteredmind.org
Teachings, articles and podcasts from Ken McLeod

Books on writing and creativity:

The Artist's Way: A Spiritual Path to Higher Creativity by Julia Cameron

Writing Down the Bones: Freeing the Writer Within by Natalie Goldberg

Writing Begins with the Breath: Embodying your Authentic Voice by Laraine Herring

Dojo Wisdom for Writers by Jennifer Lawler

Fearless Creating: A Step-by-step Guide to Starting and Completing your Work of Art by Eric Maisel

About the Author

Jessica Davidson started life as a musician and sound engineer. She has been a clerical serf, labelled library books, counselled addicts, toured Europe with an orchestra, produced demos for rock bands, and recorded a talking newspaper for a local council. She began writing in an effort to make sense of it all.

Her novel, *Addled: Adventures of a Reluctant Mystic*, was inspired by her experience of awakening, and is rooted in the philosophy of Zen Buddhism. Available from Amazon.

She lives in her head, but can usually be found in the UK.

Visit her website: **www.jessicadavidson.co.uk**

62520061R00141